Justice and Liberty

by
D. D. RAPHAEL

The Athlone Press
LONDON

First published 1980 by
THE ATHLONE PRESS
at 90–91 Great Russell Street, London WC1
The Athlone Press is an imprint
of Bemrose UK Limited

Distributor in U.S.A. and Canada
Humanities Press Inc
New Jersey

British Library Cataloguing in Publication Data
Raphael, David Daiches
Justice and liberty.
1. Liberty   2. Justice
I. Title
323.44   JC585
ISBN 0 485 11195 0

Set in Monotype Imprint by
GLOUCESTER TYPESETTING CO LTD
Gloucester

Printed in Great Britain by
WESTERN PRINTING SERVICES LTD
Bristol

Preface

The essays collected in this book were written for separate occasions but they have close connections with each other. I have been asked on a number of occasions, by scholars on both sides of the Atlantic, to put together some of the earlier papers, originally published in learned journals; and when I have delivered more recent ones as lectures at conferences and the like, they too have prompted inquiries about publication. The interest has extended as much to the historical as to the systematic discussions, and indeed I think that political philosophy benefits from combining the two. There is less certainty of benefit from combining the thoughts of youth and middle age, but several of the later essays do in fact develop themes suggested in earlier ones.

Justice and liberty are the central concepts of social and political thought. The ideological differences between political parties depend largely on differing interpretations given to the ideas of justice and liberty, and on the comparative weight attached to each when we have to choose between them. There is often a real conflict between liberty and the equalitarian aspect of justice. This is generally recognized, though people differ about the details. In some parts of the book I have tried to clarify the conflict. It is less often recognized, however, that justice and liberty have some important things in common, and I have laid more stress on this.

The idea of liberty or freedom is obviously one which puts the individual first in the scale of values. It stands up for the individual against the State or other collectivity. Justice on the other hand is more of a social value. It is concerned to maintain order in society and to preserve or secure fairness as between different individuals and groups. But justice is also the champion of the individual against the collectivity. It is ready to oppose claims of the general interest on the ground that individuals have rights which should often prevail over the interest of the community at large. For this reason I maintain that there is a basic identity in the aims of justice and liberty. The identity depends on a common source in the foundation of ethics, the idea of persons as ends-in-themselves. This (Kantian) conception of ethics shows up deficiencies in the rival theory of utilitarianism, and I believe that the conflict which does exist between liberty and equalitarian justice is less important than the conflict which is apt to arise between justice and utility. In that latter conflict liberty stands allied with justice.

The basic identity which I see between justice and liberty is, I think, the most distinctive thesis in the essays which make up this book. But there are a couple of others which should perhaps also be mentioned. Both of them arose as early as Essay 1, published in 1946. They have been elaborated in some of my later writings (both in essays reprinted here and in books). One is an explanation of the connection in socialist thought between a needs concept of justice and an equalitarian concept. Discrimination in favour of need is an unequal distribution, but its purpose is to try to make up for an existing inequality and so it uses unequal distribution as a means to the end of promoting equality. The other is a conceptual distinction between the right to do something, as an absence of obligation, and the right to receive something, as correlative to the presence of an obligation on the part of others.

Most, but not all, of the essays are revised (in one instance, much expanded) versions of articles previously published as follows: Essay 1, *Philosophy*, 1946; 2, *The General Election in Glasgow, February 1950*, ed. S. B. Chrimes (1950); 3 and 10, *Proceedings of the Aristotelian Society*, 1950–1 and 1972–3; 4, *Equality and Freedom*, ed. G. Dorsey (Oceana Publications, Inc., 1977); 5, *Political Studies*, 1964; 6, *Revue Internationale de Philosophie*, 1979; 7 and part of 8, *Mind*, 1974 and 1979; 11, in Italian translation, *Rivista Internazionale di Filosofia del Diritto*, 1977. Essay 9 has not been published before.

1979   D.D.R.

Contents

1 Equality and Equity

In some sense every man has a moral right, or more properly a moral claim, to equality with other men. In what sense will, I hope, become apparent in the course of this essay. That there is such a claim in some sense is clear enough. 'Equality before the law', for example, is something which we all recognize to be right.

It should also be clear that the moral right or claim to equality is not to be derived from considerations of utility. Although Bentham thought that all duties and rights became so purely because they increased happiness, he was obliged to add the principle 'Everybody to count for one, nobody for more than one'. The pleasure principle alone would not enable us to decide between two actions, one of which gave to one man twice the amount of pleasure that the other gave to each of two men. The utilitarians held that in choosing between these two actions a man must regard as his duty the second, the action which will produce happiness for a greater number of people, although the total amount of happiness produced by it is no greater than that produced by the first action which achieves the happiness for a lesser number of people. The utilitarian principle according to J. S. Mill is to produce the greatest possible amount of happiness for the greatest possible number. This statement in fact contains two principles, not one. Mill is saying that we have two basic duties, first to produce the greatest possible amount of happiness we can, and secondly to distribute that happiness among as many people as we can. The second, it should be noted, is not merely an extension of the happiness principle, though Mill may have thought it was. It will not do to say that by spreading happiness more widely we increase it and 'make a happier world'. The hypothesis was that two actions were open to an agent, each of which would produce in total the *same* amount of happiness. If it were true that the spreading of happiness more widely always caused an increase in the total amount of happiness, then it would be unnecessary to add to the principle of maximizing happiness by saying that our duty is *also* to produce happiness for the greatest possible number. If the widest possible distribution of happiness necessarily increased the total amount of happiness, then the way to produce the greatest possible amount of happiness would include the spreading of happiness among the greatest number of people. Our basic duty would merely be to produce the greatest possible amount of happiness, and this would give the reason for the *derivative* duty of distributing happiness as widely as possible. Producing happiness for as many people as possible would be a *means* to the end of producing as much happiness as possible; it would not itself be part of the end. Most people would in fact not say that distributing happiness widely necessarily increases its total amount, and many might even feel that sometimes wider distribution diminishes the total amount of happiness so that a conflict arises between the duty of producing the greatest possible amount of happiness and the duty of producing happiness for the greatest possible number of people. 'Everybody to count for one, nobody for more than one' is an addition to the utilitarian principle. It is justice (or rather, one element of justice) stealing back after Bentham has tried to explain it away in terms of the pleasure principle:

expellas furca tamen usque recurrit.

Nobody to count for more than one. In my duty to provide happiness for others I must, *prima facie*, distribute it equally to each man. Each man has a right to an equal share of the store of happiness which I have at my disposal.

ii

To say that a person 'has a right' may mean either of two things. First, the expression may mean that it is not wrong for the person to do or have that which he is said to have a right to do or have. 'I have a perfect right to wear brown shoes if I want to' means 'It is not wrong for me to wear brown shoes', that is, 'I am not under any obligation to refrain from wearing brown shoes'. Conversely, 'You have no right to whip that child' means, 'It is wrong for you to whip that child', that is, 'You *are* under an obligation to refrain from whipping the child'.

Secondly, to say that a person has a right may mean that someone else has an obligation to him. 'I have a right to the money you borrowed' means 'You are under an obligation to give back to me the money you borrowed'. 'That child has a right not to be whipped' means that other people have an obligation to refrain from whipping the child. A right in this second and more frequent sense is a right *against* someone, it refers to a claim which someone is obliged to fulfil. The person who is obliged to fulfil the claim may have other obligations, too, which conflict with this one. His duty is to carry out the strongest of the conflicting obligations, to satisfy the strongest claim. It will be convenient to reserve the name of 'a right' to that claim which corresponds to the strongest obligation. If we use language in this way, a claim is correlative to an obligation[1] and a right correlative to a duty. Every man may have a claim against me for equal treatment, but the claim becomes a right only if it does not conflict with some stronger claim which I am also obliged to fulfil if I can. Thus my obligation to treat A equally with B may be outweighed by an additional obligation to B arising, for example, from a contract or from a special relation of guardianship. If, for instance, I owe B a debt, if I have made a promise to him, or if I have special responsibilities towards him because he is my child, then the total obligation which I have to B is greater than that which I have to A. In this essay I am not primarily concerned, however, with choosing between conflicting claims or with the circumstances in which the claim to equality becomes a right. What I wish to discuss is the *claim* to equality, the obligation or responsibility or '*prima facie* duty' to treat all men equally.

A claim may be a claim against a particular person or particular group of persons (as with a promise or a debt) or a claim against everyone (as with the claim of the child not to be hurt, or as with the claim to be told the truth). When we say that Jones has a claim to the money which Brown has promised him or has borrowed, we are referring to the same situation as we refer to when we say that Brown has an obligation to pay the money to Jones. A man's claim against everyone, as with the claim to be told the truth, is the other side of the obligation which everyone has to him, in this case to tell him the truth. Now these claims which a man has against everyone are general not only as obligations but also as claims. Not only has Jones a claim that everyone should tell him the truth (i.e. not only has everyone the obligation to tell the truth to Jones), but everyone has this claim (i.e. everyone is obliged to tell the truth to everyone). Thus there are certain claims, correlative to certain obligations, which every man has against every other man. The claim to equality is an example of such a general claim.

iii

As soon as anyone maintains that there is a claim to equality, he is sure to be met by opponents who point to examples of countless situations in which it is obviously right to treat people *un*equally. Few persons would say that a hard-working man ought to have no more money than an idler. 'But still we know', says F. W. Maitland in his essay on 'Liberty and Equality',[2] 'that there is a general argument against inequality . . . an argument admitted every time that our Court of Chancery says that equality is equity.' This suggests that equality, in the sense in which there is a claim to it, is the same thing as equity. John Laird, however, in his book *The Device of Government* (1944), while agreeing that there is a claim to equity, thinks that equity is a different thing from equality. 'Most equalitarian arguments', he says, 'are about equity rather than about equality, and seldom do much more than warn us against arbitrary, that is, against inequitable inequality.'[3] Laird seems to be saying that there is not really any claim to equality; what there is a claim to is a different thing, equity. The arguments usually put forward against inequality are really, he says, arguments against a particular kind of inequality, inequitable inequality. According to Laird, equitable inequality is right and inequitable inequality wrong. He thus distinguishes between equality and equity, while Maitland seems to think that equality is the same as equity and therefore right or just. Leslie Stephen evidently took the same view as Maitland when he said 'The real force with which we have to reckon is the demand for justice and for equality as somehow implied by justice.'[4]

All would agree that equity is somehow connected with justice. In ordinary speech we refer to equity as 'fairness', and to say that something is unfair is either to say or to imply that it is unjust. We must now ask what is that equity or fairness, which Maitland and Leslie Stephen think is the same as equality and which Laird thinks is different. Inequality is not equitable, says Laird, if it is 'arbitrary', but he does not tell us what constitutes arbitrariness. Leslie Stephen also says that 'the revolutionary demand for equality was, historically speaking, a protest against arbitrary inequality'.[5] But preceding this remark he takes us a good deal further. 'Justice', he says, 'implies essentially indifference to irrelevant considerations, and therefore, in many cases, equality in the treatment of the persons concerned. A judge has to decide without reference to bribes, and not be biassed by the position of an accused person. In that sense he treats the men equally, but of course he does not give equal treatment to the criminal and innocent, to the rightful and wrongful claimant.'[6]

The same notion of 'relevance' is stressed in an interesting paper by G. L. Schwartz called 'Planning and Economic Privilege' and bearing the sub-title 'The Notion of Equity in Economics'.[7] Schwartz there enunciates and illustrates the dictum, 'Equality is never absolute, but may perhaps be defined as the absence of discrimination for reasons which are felt to be irrelevant.' Now the definition offered is a negative definition and, it seems to me, pre-supposes that which it purports to define. 'Discrimination' can only mean unequal treatment, so the definition tells us that equality is the absence of inequality that is based on irrelevant reasons, or in other words that equality is qualified equality, the qualification being inequality on relevant grounds. Schwartz cannot really mean that equality *is* qualified equality; his view must be that what people mean when they claim 'equality' is 'qualified equality', an equality which is qualified by inequality based on relevant grounds. And this must mean that there is a general claim to equality which is overridden in certain circumstances by reasons which are relevant to unequal treatment.

Now how do we know whether a reason adduced for unequal treatment is a relevant reason or not? Take, for example, the position of a civil servant administering some rule. He has to apply it equally to all and sundry, but he must be ready to give exceptional treatment to exceptional cases. The burden of a considerable pro-portion of Parliamentary Questions and other inquiries relating to the actions of Government Departments is to show that a particular case is exceptional and should not be bound by the ordinary rules. The rules must, it is agreed, be equally applied to all cases save those containing exceptional features which justify different treatment. But what is an exceptional feature justifying different treatment? If Tom Jones has an exceptionally long nose, can he therefore claim exceptionally large unemployment benefit? No, we are told, the unusual feature must be relevant to the issue. Again, the fact that Bill Brown is an exceptionally charming man may incline us to feel that we should like the request which he makes to be granted, but we cannot regard his exceptional charm as justifying exceptional treatment; that would be discrimination on grounds of purely personal bias. If Mrs. Smith, who is asking for an extra milk ration, brings a certificate from her doctor to say that owing to ill-health she needs more milk, that need is relevant to her request for exceptional treatment. The fact that she specially likes milk, although in one sense this is certainly *relevant* to her request for more milk, is not relevant in the sense of justifying exceptional treatment.

How then is such relevance to be determined? I suggest that the considerations which are 'relevant' to a claim for inequality are *moral* considerations, they are special moral claims. Mrs. Smith's special need gives rise to a special moral claim. A person who is in unusual need has an unusual claim. A man who has been injured has a claim to my assistance. Again, special merit may give rise to a special claim. A man who has done some special public service, like risking his life in military service during a war, has a special claim on the gratitude of the community.

The fact that special claims conflict with and override the claim to equality does not of course imply that the claim to equality has no existence or no force in such circumstances. To think that it does is to confuse a claim with a right, and an obligation (in the sense explained on p. 3 and note 1) with a duty. As was pointed out earlier, *any* claim and its corresponding obligation may be outweighed in a particular situation by another and conflicting claim, and the strongest claim becomes a right which it is a duty to satisfy. But the claim which is overridden still exists as a claim. When Schwartz says 'Equality is never absolute', he is merely saying of one claim what is true of all. No claim is absolute, that is, no claim has absolute stringency such that we can say *a priori* that it must override any conflicting claim, or any aggregate of conflicting claims, in any circumstances. The fact that the claim to equality may be overridden in particular circumstances by conflicting claims is just what we should expect. If everyone has a claim against me for equal treatment, and if one person has an *additional* (it must be additional since the claim to equality is universal) special claim against me because he is a member of my family or because he has earned my gratitude or for any other reason, then obviously his claims outweigh the single claims of others.

Unequal treatment, then, is justified when the general claim to equality is overridden by an additional special claim. Unequal treatment that is not based on a special moral claim is unjust. Now if there were no general claim to equality, as Laird seems to think, unequal treatment that was not based on a special moral claim would not be wrong, it would be morally indifferent. In order to be morally *right* unequal treatment must be based on a special moral claim or obligation, but if there were no such claim the unequal treatment, while it would certainly not be morally right,[8] would not be morally wrong but would be morally neutral or indifferent. In fact we usually find that discrimination on 'irrelevant' grounds, i.e. on grounds other than moral grounds, is not morally indifferent but is morally wrong. Consequently there must be a *prima facie* claim to equality to make unequal treatment, unless based on some additional moral claim, wrong.

iv

We have seen that Laird was mistaken in thinking, as he apparently did, that there is no claim to equality. It may be objected, however, that all he intended was the view that there is no constant *right* to equality. We have already agreed that there is no constant right to equality or to any other of the things to which we have a claim. But if this is what Laird meant, he must also have meant that there *is* a constant right to equity, that our claim to equitable treatment is always a right. This could only be the case if equity included *all* obligations, if in fact equitable action were synonymous with right action. To use 'equity' and 'equitable' in that way would obviously be unnatural and incorrect. The obligation to promote good is never thought of as an obligation required by equity or justice. Consider, again, the obligations of carrying out a promise, of paying a debt, of telling the truth, of providing special benefits for one's family or one's friends; we should indeed say that some of these obligations are a part of justice, but we should not say they are required by equity or fairness. When Laird suggests that equitable inequality is right and inequitable inequality wrong, his view is incorrect whether he is referring to claims or to constant rights. If we are speaking of claims, there is a claim to equality unqualified by equity or anything else. If we are speaking of rights, there is no constant right to equity unqualified in any circumstances. The claim to equality may be qualified by the claims of equity, and similarly it, and the claims of equity, may be qualified by other obligations.

Nevertheless there is, as shown by the quotations on pp. 4–5 from Maitland and Leslie Stephen as well as by the quotation from Laird, some closer connection between equality and equity than between equality and the other things which may qualify it. To discover what this connection is, let us consider those claims which qualify equality in the name of equity or fairness. Take, for instance, the policy of the British Government, at the end of the Second World War, on the question of demobilization from the Forces. The principle of equality said 'First in, first out'. That principle was modified by the criterion of age because it was thought that military service and absence from home are a greater hardship for the old than for the young. 'It is only fair', people said, to shorten the service of the older men. That was a concession, on grounds of equity or fairness, to the claim of hardship or need. Again, many people thought that the Government's scheme should be modified so as to give some degree of preference to men who had served overseas. This[9] was a claim on grounds of desert or merit, and again it was thought to be fair or equitable to make such a modification. Although the Government did not include this modification in their scheme, they did not deny that it would have been equitable to do so. What they said was that equity must give way to simplicity, to utility in fact, which shows that utility and equity have to compete as conflicting claims and that equity sometimes has to give way. With these proposed modifications of the strictly equalitarian scheme of 'First in, first out' may be contrasted the modification of early release for building workers, a special Class B in the Government's scheme. Nobody would say that it was *fair* to let out first the building workers who went in last. The reason for letting them out first was a utilitarian reason. They were to be released 'in the national interest', that is, because of the benefit which they were expected to confer on the community. (It may be said that this also was a case of need. 'The community needed them.' All the same it was not a matter of equity. The relation of this claim of general need, as compared with the claim of individual need, to equality and equity will be considered later.)

I propose to examine the following types of case in which inequality of treatment seems to be called for, and which are often used as arguments against the existence of a claim to equality. They are (1) the claim of need or hardship, to which corresponds the principle of distribution 'To everyone according to his needs', (2) the claim of desert, to which corresponds the principle 'To everyone according to his merit', (3) the claim of natural capacity, to which corresponds the principle 'To everyone according to his ability', and (4) the claim of public welfare, to which corresponds the utilitarian principle of acting so as to maximize happiness. I have suggested that (1) and (2) are connected with equity, and that (4) is not (though we have to consider the relation of (4), looked at from the aspect of public need, to (1)). Many people would say that (3) is an equitable principle, and because of this and of the frequency with which (3) is used as an argument against equalitarianism, I think it, too, should be examined with the others. I do not propose to consider inequality of distribution based on other types of claim, such as the claim of a promise or a debt, or the claims of family and friends, because I think it is sufficiently clear by now what their relation is to the claim of equality and because it is also clear that they are not claims required by equity.

V

1. First let us take the example of special need. The grant of a special allowance of petrol, at a time when petrol is scarce and must be rationed, can be justified by a special need for petrol. If I am a farmer dwelling in a remote district who cannot earn my living without having a car in which to travel to the market town, I may claim discriminatory treatment. But what I am really claiming is *equal* treatment. I am saying that unless special means are taken to

B

provide me with a conveyance, I shall receive *less* good treatment than most people, who live where there are public transport services. My need would be equally well met by the provision of a public transport service in my district. So long as I am at a disadvantage as compared with most people, equity demands that I receive special treatment to remedy the disadvantage. But in doing so equity is not overriding equality. The claim of equity in these circumstances is a claim for equality, not for inequality. There appears to be inequality only because the means required in these circumstances to give me equal treatment with other people is *different* from that employed for the other people. I am not given greater advantages than they in the matter of benefiting from mechanical transport; the discrimination is an attempt to give me *equal* advantages, but because of my peculiar circumstances I have to receive those equal advantages by different methods from those used in towns. Townspeople are provided with public transport services, the institution of which in my district would be uneconomical, and therefore I am enabled to use a car of my own. Discrimination on grounds of special need is an attempt to achieve equality by what appears at first sight to be unequal treatment. It is an attempt to remove inequality arising from extraneous causes. The man who lives in the remote highlands is at a disadvantage, as compared with the townsman, in the matter of access to transport. The man who is disabled is at a disadvantage, as compared with the fit, in the matter of getting a job and living comfortably. The child who is mentally backward is at a disadvantage as compared with the mentally alert. Discrimination on grounds of special need is therefore not a limitation of equality but an attempt to help achieve it.[10] In so far as equity demands special allowance for special need, equity does not depart from equality.

2. The second type of special claim justifying discrimination which we proposed to examine is desert or merit. The man who has specially benefited the community deserves more than his neighbours in the communal distribution of happiness. It may be said that there is some connection with equality here also. The idea seems to be, in part at any rate, that equal services should be equally rewarded and unequal services unequally. In origin the special claim of desert may have arisen from the claim to equality. The underlying thought may have been that if a man has given

benefit to others he should receive equal value in return to make up, as it were, for the loss that he has voluntarily incurred; and the man who has taken from others should suffer an equal loss in requital. The idea may have been to level up the inequalities caused by human actions, as the special allowances for special needs are attempts to level up the inequalities due to extraneous causes. However, this relation to equality does not now give desert its special moral claim. The man who has been disabled by fighting for his country is thought to have a double claim, the claim of need and the claim of merit, and so to have a stronger claim to special treatment than the man who has been disabled from birth.[11]

The difference may be illustrated by considering the claim of compensation, which is what we suggested may have given rise originally to the claim of desert. The man who has been injured by the negligent action of a motorist or an employer has a claim against the motorist or employer for compensation, which is supposed to be equal in value to the loss which he has sustained. His claim is to be requited to the extent of the loss. There is more than this in the case of merit. The disabled ex-serviceman is not thought of as *merely* having a claim of compensation against the community, for whose sake he suffered his disability. Gratitude for the benefit which he has given or intended by his sacrifice, and admiration for the voluntary nature of the sacrifice, are added. The *merit* is in fact constituted by the intention of conferring benefit and the voluntary readiness to suffer. The ex-serviceman who is not disabled has not so strong a claim as the ex-serviceman who is disabled, because he is not in special need, but he is still thought to have the special claim of merit for his readiness to suffer and for his having conferred, or having intended to confer, benefit on the community.

In the case of special need we saw that the apparent inequality of treatment which equity requires is in fact an attempt to produce equality, to make up for the inequality which is shown in unequal needs. The unequal treatment required for special desert, however, is a real deviation from equality. 'To each according to his needs' is therefore a more equalitarian doctrine than 'To each according to his merit'. Ordinary moral consciousness requires the satisfaction of both claims.

3. Let us now consider the third example of special capacity. If the State provides scholarships and grants for university courses,

it should not give them to all children but only to those who are capable of benefiting from a university education. But all children (save those few who are morons) are capable of benefiting from *some* kind of education, and therefore the State is regarded as having the obligation to provide all with some kind of education. The ideal that is pursued is to provide each child with that kind of education to which its natural abilities are suited. As the opponents of equality are quick to point out, men are by no means equal in their natural capacities, and the principle of distributing the opportunity for development in accordance with natural capacity appears to be a principle of inequality.

It should be noted that the essential part of the distribution in this case is not the distribution of means to present enjoyment but the distribution of opportunity, of potential means to enjoyment. In so far as everyone enjoys such exercise of his natural capacities as he is capable of making, the provision of education or training in accordance with capacity is a provision of present enjoyment. If a child who has no aptitude for mathematics but has an aptitude for craftsmanship is forced to go to a grammar school and learn mathematics, his actual education will be disagreeable to him. Apprentice him to an artisan who will teach him to exercise and develop his aptitude for craftsmanship, and he will enjoy his schooling. Education in accordance with capacity does, then, give present enjoyment in the exercise of natural abilities, and it is obviously the best way of distributing such enjoyment as equally as possible since it is to be presumed that one child enjoys the exercise of his particular bent as much as another enjoys the exercise of his. This would hardly be disputed. But the inequality comes in, it would be said, in the future enjoyment to which the education is a means. Since men differ in their capacities, development according to capacity must also be different for different people and so lead to different occupations or lives. Education in a grammar school is likely to lead to a non-manual occupation. Education in a technical school is likely to lead to the life of an artisan. Thus the distribution of opportunity to exercise and develop natural capacity in accordance with the kind of capacity one has, is an equal distribution of present enjoyment but a differentiated distribution of the means to future enjoyment.

I have said that the distribution of the means to future enjoyment, if based on natural capacity, in which men differ, is a differentiated distribution; I have not said it is an unequal distribution. Of course men are not equal in their capacities, and therefore distribution according to capacity is, it would seem, unequal distribution. But what do we mean when we say men are unequal in their natural capacities? In order to say this we must look at particular capacities. Bill Brown has more brain power than Tom Smith, but Tom Smith may be physically stronger than Bill Brown. We say they are unequal and we imply that one has more than the other. But they are not unequal in natural capacity *simpliciter*. It would be nonsense, or at any rate highly misleading, to say that Brown has more natural capacity than Smith. We could say he has more capac*ities* than Smith if Smith happened to lack one of the capacities that most men have, e.g. if Smith were blind or paralysed. When we say that Brown and Smith are unequal in capacity, we must specify what capacity we are talking about. Men certainly *differ* in capacity, but to say they are *unequal* in capacity is to speak in a vague and misleading way.

Of course people who speak of inequality of natural capacity are usually thinking of the inequality of earning power which different capacities bring. If a boy is born with more than average brains and is given a university education, he is likely to earn more money than his neighbour. But greater intellectual ability does not necessarily bring a larger income. A good craftsman may earn more than a teacher, and a champion boxer more than a scientist; then the greater earning power goes to the greater capacity for craftsmanship or physical strength, not to the keener intellect. In a society in which there were healthy conditions and decent education for all, there would still be few qualified to be scientists, but there would also be few whose capacities would be used to the full by employment as labourers or porters; and it would then be necessary to make labouring, especially in unpleasant work such as sewage disposal, sufficiently attractive to be taken up by offering for it a higher wage than would be offered for a more congenial job. The distribution of different kinds of education according to different capacities is not of itself an unequal distribution of the means to future enjoyment. The inequality arises from other factors in the economic system. A grammar school education for a boy who is better at mathematics than at handicrafts does not in itself provide him with greater opportunity for future means to happiness than does a technical school education or an industrial apprenticeship for a boy whose abilities lie in that direction. The inequality of opportunity arises from features of the economic system. In our pre-war economic system a skilled worker in industry was paid less than a clerk. If at the present time a skilled worker in industry is paid as much as, or more than, a clerk, the inequality no longer exists or works the other way. At any rate the difference in the two types of education is not a case of inequality, nor need it lead to inequality. The provision of educational opportunity according to type of ability provides differentiated but not unequal opportunity, and equality is not qualified by taking account of differences of ability.

We have found that in the distribution of opportunity for development of natural capacity, the present exercise of abilities called forth by the process of development should, so far as possible, give enjoyment and give it equally, while the future exercise of abilities which is made possible by the development should be differentiated (a qualitative, not a quantitative, distinction and so not involving inequality) according to the type of natural capacity. The actual differentiation, the qualitative distinction, is not required by equity but by a different ethical principle, the principle of beneficence.[12] To give someone opportunities to exercise and develop a capacity in which he is particularly apt is to give him happiness (since the exercise of the capacity is pleasant) and the means to happiness (since he will probably be able to earn his living by turning the developed capacity to use); to fail to give him those opportunities is to neglect the obligation of providing happiness which it was possible to provide; to make him try to develop capacities in which he has small potentiality is to make him do something which is painful in itself and which will lead to no beneficial, and probably to harmful, results since the training is going to be of no use to him and is likely to block the development of other capacities in which he has greater potentiality.

4. Let us consider, fourthly, whether the principle of equality is qualified by discrimination on grounds of public welfare. The State may subsidize scientific research and thus provide a group of research workers with a fair-sized salary. A taxpayer who is not one of the immediate beneficiaries of the subsidy might complain that

this is discriminatory distribution of public funds. But the *reason* for the discriminatory distribution is not to benefit the scientists Jones and Robinson while neglecting the clerk Brown and the labourer Smith. The subsidy is provided in order that the discoveries of the scientists may help to advance the general prosperity of the country and so lead eventually to a higher standard of life for *all* its inhabitants.[13] It is designed to benefit all members of the community indiscriminately and so (as far as can be foreseen or provided for) equally.

Nevertheless, although the ultimate purpose is non-discrimination, the immediate effect is discrimination. The moral principle which justifies this departure from equality of distribution is not equity. Nobody says that it is *fair* to give subsidies to scientists. Equity requires that the eventual greater prosperity which is expected to be obtained should, when available, be equally distributed to all the members of the community, but does not require the making of efforts to obtain extra wealth to be distributed. Equity relates only to the *method of distributing* goods which are actually available for distribution. The obligation to seek to obtain or produce further goods for distribution is one enjoined by the general obligation of beneficence.

We can now return to the suggestion made earlier that discrimination on grounds of public benefit may also be regarded as made on grounds of need. If the particular public benefit which is sought is one which will not simply add to positive happiness but will remove or reduce existing unhappiness, or is one which is felt to be essential before life can be called decently happy, we say it is a public need. Early release from the Forces of building operatives was said to be a public need because of the evils of overcrowded and insanitary accommodation: early release from the Forces of schoolteachers was also regarded by many people as a public need because they felt that better education for their children was indispensable to civilized life. The claim of need in such circumstances, however, is not a special claim of particular individuals but a general claim of all or nearly all. The distinction between particular claims of individuals and general claims which everybody has was explained earlier. The general obligation (i.e. the obligation incumbent on each and every man) to maximize the happiness of others and minimize their unhappiness has as its correlative a general claim. This general obligation and its correlative claim are what the utilitarians were after in their pleasure principle (though they failed to see that the obligation is not to produce happiness as such but to produce it for other people). The combination of this general obligation with the general obligation to distribute equally the happiness available for distribution gives us the utilitarian system of ethics. By restricting their ethics to these two principles, however, the utilitarians were guilty of over-simplification including insufficient attention to the particular or special obligations which may modify the application of general obligations.

vi

We have considered four types of case in which there appeared to be rightful inequality in the distribution of benefit. We found that in the first, discrimination on grounds of special need, the apparent inequality of distribution was really an attempt to achieve equality or at any rate less inequality; that in the second, discrimination on grounds of special desert, there was real inequality; that in the third, provision of opportunity for development according to capacity, there was not in fact unequal distribution but differentiated distribution; and that in the fourth type of case, discrimination on grounds of public welfare, there was unequal distribution of existing goods with the aim of distributing equally the goods which it was hoped to produce in the future as a consequence of the present distribution. We found that it was equity which made the distribution in the first two types of case right, but that it was not equity or justice but the separate obligation of beneficence which was responsible for the rightness of the initial distribution in the third and fourth types of case. Equity requires inequality of initial distribution (a) to meet special need, in order to achieve real equality, and (b) to meet special desert.

Apart from the case of desert, therefore, equity requires equality. In all other cases where equity appears to qualify equality, it is in fact ensuring that the execution of the principle of equality shall not be a wooden execution that defeats its own object. Utilitarians would say that discrimination on grounds of desert is for the sake of future good and so not demanded by equity but by the obligation of beneficence. I do not myself think that the utilitarian analysis of the claim of desert is correct. It seems to me that the claim of desert is a part of justice or equity, and that in this one type of case equity qualifies equality. That the principle of equality is a part of equity and not a separate principle is, I think, obvious not merely from the fact that the claim of equity to justify discrimination in favour of special need is a claim for equality, but also because discrimination (i.e. divergence from equality) which is not based on moral grounds is thought of not simply as wrong but as *unfair*; if the special case of desert is subtracted, fairness means equality.

Our conclusion, then, is that equity includes the claim of equality and the claim of desert. It is in fact the same as distributive justice. Maitland was wrong in suggesting that equality is the same as equity, but it is the larger part of equity. Laird was wrong in suggesting that equity and equality are opposed, for equity includes equality. Leslie Stephen was right in saying that equality is implied by justice, for equality forms part of distributive justice.

2 Freedom and Fair Shares: the Issues of an Election[1]

INTRODUCTORY

Comparatively few electors decide which way to vote on the specific issues that are presented to them as paramount at a particular election. Equally few electors are fully-fledged members of a political party, but most people have a fairly definite bias of support or dislike for the political creed, however vaguely conceived, of one of the two main parties. The 'floating vote' is relatively small. Parliamentary candidates know that for all the tub-thumping, the heckling, the excitement, the hectic outpouring of nervous energy in the campaign, the only votes to be won over are those described, unkindly and unfairly, as ready to 'float' from one side to the other. Yet our electoral system is such that this fairly small collection of flotsam can sharply tip out the occupants of the governmental canoe and ensure a smooth passage for the new crew. Although the particular issues of a particular election have little influence in determining the vast majority of votes, they do often determine the outcome of the election.

Here we shall be concerned with the issues of the election of 1950 as they were presented in Glasgow, by the election addresses of the candidates, by the speeches of candidates and their supporters, by the party literature (national, regional, and local) distributed to the homes of electors and to the hands of those attending meetings. These sources show how the issues were presented to electors, and what issues the parties thought important. But the British electorate is not a sponge that simply absorbs party propaganda. The issues as the elector sees them are not necessarily the issues as the party presents them. The differences are small and should not be exaggerated. But it would be a mistake to assume that they do not exist. One impression given by the mass of material collected in our survey is that nationalization—undoubtedly the chief issue in much Conservative literature—fell rather flat with the Glasgow electorate. The other main Conservative issue, the cost of living, was far more important to the voters. How is one to gauge the mind of the electorate on issues? Our information on that point is scanty, compared with the flood of oratory and leaflets poured out by the parties on *their* view of the issues. For this reason one can say little about the mind of the electorate, and that little must be stamped with a rubric of caution. But the questions asked at meetings are some guide (after making allowance for the fact that the majority of questions at election meetings are put by hostile individuals who have come to embarrass the candidate, or by cliques and claques out to make the proceedings lively). The frequency, perhaps unexpected,—as in the case of Post-War Credits—with which a topic is raised in questions shows what issues chiefly exercise the electors, at any rate of a particular region. At least it shows what corner of their shoes is pinching the hardest, and after all, the pinching of the average citizen's shoes should be eased by government if possible and is therefore one type of political issue. But are questioners at meetings representative of the general electorate? Only the merest fraction of voters attend meetings, and of those who do many have already made up their minds and come to meetings not for enlightenment but to show solidarity or to have a bit of fun. Still, honest doubters are there too. One of our observers made a point of conversing with a few members of the audience at every meeting he attended. He was told more than once by those whom he buttonholed that they were rather disillusioned with the Labour Government and were coming along to meetings in order to make up their minds which way they should vote this time. These are genuine floating voters, and their questions to candidates, or their overheard remarks, are some indication of why and whether they were likely to change their recent allegiance.

We can, then, paint a pretty clear picture of the issues as presented by the candidates and parties, and can add a few cautious and hesitant touches to delineate the issues apparently prominent in the minds of electors. Our picture refers to Glasgow. To what extent is Glasgow typical? Mr. Walter Elliot was reported in the *Glasgow Herald* of 27 January as saying, at his adoption meeting, that 'Clydeside would be the cockpit of the electoral struggle'. Where the fight is sharpest the opposing sides make the best of their weapons, but these may not necessarily be the same weapons as those used elsewhere. Agricultural issues, for instance, played no part in Glasgow. While may of the issues in this city were doubtless similar to those of other large industrial towns, still Glasgow rightly prides itself on unique features. It is the hub of Clydeside, where ships and engines are built for all nations. It suffered more than any town from the great depression between the wars, and the iron bitterness of those days has entered deeply into its memories, responsible above all else for the colour of 'the Red Clyde'. It is Scottish, containing one fifth of the population of Scotland, and is, despite its industrial character, not insensitive to the independent feeling of the Scots. Even the Redness, or rather Pinkness, of the Clyde is pretty independent and non-conformist. Glasgow was for many years a stronghold of the Independent Labour Party, and the sombre photograph of Jimmy Maxton in the shop-window of the I.L.P. Committee Rooms at Bridgeton, urging passers-by to 'Be Faithful to Old Faithful', symbolized a spirit that lingers still even in those candidates (and their supporters) who formerly belonged to the I.L.P. and had now gone over to the majority party; their policies were by no means wholly those of official Labour. Again, the citizens of Glasgow include a fair number of Irish birth or descent, who feel strongly about the problems of Ireland. Some of the issues in Glasgow, then, are bound to be local. But none of them affects Glasgow alone. The memory of unemployment in the shipyards does not differ in kind from the memory of unemployment elsewhere, and even in degree it has its parallels in some other large industrial towns. Scottish nationalism means at least as much to the four million Scots outside Glasgow as to the one million within. The I.L.P. retains its flicker of life in a few other centres. Irishmen in Liverpool and elsewhere feel as strongly about the partition of Ireland as do those in Glasgow. In any event, local issues are the smaller part of the story. The cost of living, full employment, housing, social security, these and many more vexed questions affect all parts of Britain; and in speaking, writing, and distributing propaganda about them, Glasgow candidates naturally used the material put out from their national party headquarters. Accordingly, the election issues presented in Glasgow are largely those of the national party publications. But often the slant, the tone, the high-lighting, show up local perspective and local colour.

THE MAIN ISSUES

The initiative in casting up the issues of the election naturally lay with the challengers. The Government was on the whole content to point to its record and ask to be allowed to continue its work. Several Labour speakers claimed that this was the only Government to have fulfilled all its promises, the chief of them being full employment and social security. The party manifesto, *Let Us Win Through Together*, retails with pride the record of its achievements, and of these, two were singled out: 'The Labour Government has ensured full employment and fair shares of the necessities of life.' The pamphlet goes on: 'No doubt there have been mistakes. But judge on what basis you will—by the standard of life of the general body of citizens, by employment, by the infrequency of serious industrial disputes, by the stability of the nation, by social security —by any fair comparison, the British people have done an infinitely better job than was done after the first World War.' A little booklet giving *Fifty Facts for Labour* points the moral on its last page: 'Labour has earned its second term.' Nor was this feeling absent from the minds of the electorate. 'These politicians are all the same', said a working-class housewife from Clydebank, giving expression to a traditional attitude; 'we do the work and they get the money. I have never voted before. It's a waste of time. But still,' she added, 'I think the Labour Government has been trying to do a good job and should be allowed to carry on. So I'm going to vote this time for Labour.' And a middle-class woman was overheard to say to a Conservatively-minded companion, as they left a Conservative meeting: 'Well, *I'm* going to vote Labour. Whatever your income, you have to approve of what they've done, and I think we should let them get on with it.'

The opposition, of course, found the Labour record far from satisfying. Nationalization and Socialist finance had put the country on the rocks. The Government was far too occupied with a complacent looking-backwards. What was needed was a new look —forwards—a forward look to 1952 when Marshall Aid would end. If the dollar gap were not bridged by that time, full employment would indeed be only a thing to look back to, a thing of the past. The value of the £ must be restored, taxation reduced, and incentives increased. Enterprise was to be encouraged, not stifled and frustrated by centralized control. Nationalization was clogging, extravagant, and inefficient. Huge losses had to be borne by the taxpayer, prices were up and quality down. The financial record of Labour was pretty miserable. So, too, was its record on housing. Nationalization, finance, and housing, were the three issues put at the top of the bill by most Conservative candidates in Glasgow. Some put nationalization first, some finance.

What of the Liberals? Their leaflets and speeches insisted that the two main parties invited electors to vote *against* something, while their own policy was positive, something to vote *for*. On a number of matters they did indeed offer a positive and definite programme: co-ownership in industry, a reformed system of taxation, free trade, Proportional Representation, equality for women, the abolition of conscription, Home Rule for Scotland. But none of these proposals struck home with the electorate as a crucial issue, and one or two of them (the abolition of conscription, and perhaps the restoration of free trade) seemed dubious. Consequently the Liberal volley misfired, and their proposals took on the appearance of a list of details. In the absence of any big central issue, the force of the Liberal programme as a winner of votes was dissipated.

Foreign policy was not a major issue in the election. The Communists tried to make it so, but they preached only to the handful of converted. Mr. Churchill seems to have thought that he introduced foreign policy as an issue in his Edinburgh speech of 14 February, but the electorate in Glasgow at least was barely affected by that discussion. There was no substantial difference between the foreign policies of the Conservative and the Labour Parties.

The chief concrete issues, then, were nationalization, finance, and housing, for the Conservatives, and the Government's record, especially on employment, for Labour. Each side selected different issues, and neither was willing to meet its opponent on the ground offered. The issue of nationalization did not altogether go by default. The Labour Party leaders indeed seemed deliberately to ignore this issue, as if they were afraid of it. Some local candidates, however, put up a reasoned case in defence of past nationalization, if not of the proposals for a further instalment. But generally speaking, they did not treat nationalization as a really serious challenge to be met. The financial situation was on the whole presented by Labour as giving ground for sober optimism and not as a matter of crisis. Their housing record Labour felt to be satisfactory. On the other side the Conservatives repudiated indignantly the suggestions that they wanted unemployment and that the Labour Government had been responsible for the absence of unemployment in the period of the sellers' market after the war. None of the concrete issues, then, was fairly and squarely fought as such by both sides. Each played at shadow-boxing with an imaginary opponent. The different issues were not unconnected, of course, and the attack of each side on its chosen issues contained implicitly some defence against the charges on other subjects made by the opposing party. But there was no head-on collision in concrete issues. The direct collision was in the more abstract realm of social philosophies, in the permanent difference between Conservatism and Socialism. But the issue here was veiled and obscure, even for most of the contestants. The difference of social philosophy is not one of the issues that attracts floating votes. It reflects rather the foundations of the attached vote. By clarifying this issue we shall see why the majority of Conservative and Labour votes were cast as they were. Election propaganda did not catch these votes. It simply brought into a half-light the dim influences that slowly win and harden votes all the time, unrelated to the crises and criticisms of a particular election period.

SOCIAL PHILOSOPHIES—FREEDOM AND FAIR SHARES

Several of the Labour candidates and their supporting speakers, especially when addressing a well-educated audience, stressed the ethical and Christian nature of socialism. Mr. W. Leonard, Labour and Co-operative candidate for Woodside, wrote in a leaflet, *A Personal Message to the Electors of Woodside*: 'The Labour Party was built on the failure of the old political parties to ensure the bounties of nature to all. It is a Party of high principled men and women in all walks of life. Its ethics are those of the Sermon on the Mount.' The Rev. Dr. George MacLeod, Leader of the Iona Community, speaking in support of Labour candidates at a meeting on 17 February, was reported by the *Glasgow Herald* to say that 'there were two kinds of planning. One was planning for profits and the other was planning to get work for all. We must plan for the good of all. He was on the side of the Labour Party in the cause of love.' At the same meeting, one of the Labour candidates urged his audience to 'look beyond personal interests when voting, and to vote for the party which would give welfare and happiness to the greatest number of people'. That party, he contended, was the Labour Party. The same candidate was asked at another meeting whether the fact that Labour held political meetings on Sundays, while their opponents did not, was indicative of a difference of attitude towards religion. The candidate took up the challenge seriously. He said that it probably did indicate a difference of attitude. To the Labour Party, political activity had its ethical and spiritual side in the attempt to remove social evil, and he felt that such work was not unworthy of the spirit of Sunday. The evangelistic note was again struck by Labour speakers and pamphlets when they declared that the period of Labour government from 1945 to 1950 was 'the first chapter of a new age'. 'We are choosing', said one Labour candidate, 'between two contrasting views of life, the competitive view and the co-operative view.' An *Election Special* leaflet, distributed on behalf of Labour candidates in several constituencies, put the contrast more strongly: 'I believe that a society of greater justice and equality is being created by the Labour Government. . . . The Tory Party is wedded to a cruel and heartless system. . . . You have the opportunity to declare that our salvation does not lie in the Tory idea of "Everyone for himself," but in working together for the common good of all.'

Conservatives, too, saw the choice as one 'between two contrasting views of life', but to them the two views appeared very differently. Mr. T. C. Henderson, the Conservative candidate for Shettleston, wrote in his election address: 'The most vital issue . . . is choosing, not so much between two candidates, or two parties, but between two distinct *Ways of Life*. On the one hand the Socialist way, with its prodigality, its state monopolies, its controls, its slant towards Communism, its class warfare, its bureaucracy, and political ideologies which must be propagated regardless of the consequences. On the other hand the Unionist way, in which the greatest emphasis is on Freedom, freedom of action, freedom of choice, freedom of thought, and free economy.' Mr. Eden, speaking in St. Andrew's Hall, Glasgow, on 15 February, likewise made freedom his main theme. The *Glasgow Herald* reported: 'Turning to home affairs, Mr. Eden declared that there were three freedoms which we must vigorously pursue. The first was freedom for men or women in every walk of life to earn more by extra effort without such crippling taxation as would deprive them of their just reward. The second was freedom to own their own homes instead of being for all time tenants of the State, and the third was that freedom which would make the State the servant of the people and not their master.'

The appeal to ethics, then, was not confined to the Left. Liberty no less than social justice is an ethical claim, and has been traditionally the corner-stone of the moral claims of British democracy. The Conservative candidate for Cathcart, again recommending freedom as a 'way of life', emphasized its British character. 'The Unionist Party', he wrote in his first communication to the electors, 'is determined . . . to restore to British people the British way of life, a life in which men and women count as self-respecting individuals and not as obedient units in a State machine; . . . a life allowing freedom for the individual to use his initiative and enterprise and to reap the highest reward possible in a healthily competitive world.' That the Conservative view of life is 'the competitive view' is freely admitted here, but competition is claimed to be 'healthy' as a necessary condition of freedom.

Labour would rejoin, 'Freedom for whom?' The article in the Labour *Election Special* which said 'the Tory Party is wedded to a cruel and heartless system' also declared: 'It is an insult to our intelligence for Tories to tell the people of Britain that we could return to the old world of "freedom and the responsibility of free enterprise." I know only too well—and so do many of you—that the only freedom of the poor was the freedom to starve.' In place of this, Labour claimed that they had substituted the freedom given by a secure wage. In curtailing the sectional freedoms that had entailed lack of freedom for the masses, they had extended economic freedom to all. Mr. Attlee, speaking in St. Andrew's Hall, Glasgow, on 13 February, said that Labour had increased freedom; to political and civic freedom Labour had added economic freedom for all citizens.

But Conservatives would not accept the charge that they cared only for the freedom of a section of the population. The Conservative philosophy, they would hold, is not 'the selfish doctrine of "everyone for himself" ', a description used in a Labour election

c

address. 'As a Unionist,' wrote the candidate for Gorbals in his address, 'I strive for the balanced State in which no section of the community is subservient to the other and which allows everyone to rise according to his ability, at the same time tempering ambition with a sense of responsibility to others.' It seems to be agreed here that individual ambition, if matched by the ability to rise, should come first, but it should be tempered by social responsibility. It is in the *relative emphasis* placed on these two concepts, or their equivalents, that the essential difference between the Conservative and Labour philosophies emerges. Labour stresses 'fair shares for all' more than freedom for the individual to satisfy his personal ambition. Conservatism lays the greater stress on freedom for the individual from the State controls which, no doubt virtuously intending to promote social justice, place fetters upon initiative and are unjust in their effect. 'To-day', says the Conservative manifesto, *This is the Road*, 'all forms of production and distribution are hampered in a Socialist atmosphere which denies enterprise its reward while making life too easy for the laggards.'

The issue of social justice was introduced into the election in the guise of the slogan 'Fair Shares for All'. This appeared to be a definite social issue. Labour candidates made much use of it, and evidently regarded the policy as the prerogative of their party. Mr. Churchill at least seemed to confirm their claim, for he attacked the slogan, as meaning, in the mouth of a Socialist, equal shares for all, irrespective of effort. In his Edinburgh speech of 14 February, as reported by the *Glasgow Herald*, he said: 'The vote-catching election cry of "fair shares for all" . . . is meaningless unless it is also stated who is to be the judge of what is fair. . . . But what the average Socialist really means when he speaks of "fair shares for all" is equal shares for all—equal shares for those who toil and those who shirk.' It is, however, doubtful whether 'fair shares' *in itself* was a disputed issue between the social aims of the two parties. It seemed to be such simply because the representatives of the Labour Party did not go to the trouble of making clear (to themselves perhaps no more than to others) what *fair* shares meant. They denied Mr. Churchill's interpretation, but were unwilling or unable to deal with his alternative challenge that the slogan was meaningless without clarification. Mr. Attlee, in the last of the election broadcasts, referred to Mr. Churchill's attack and merely pointed out that the opposite of fair shares was unfair shares. Of course the Conservatives were not willing to advocate unfair shares. Their case was that Socialism produced an *unfair* dead level, 'which denies enterprise its reward while making life too easy for the laggards'. The Socialists, however, would not agree that fair shares meant a dead level. When a Labour candidate was asked whether the high salaries paid to leading officials in the nationalized industries were consistent with the Labour policy of fair shares, he replied that fair shares were not equal shares; salaries depended partly on degree of responsibility. Sir Stafford Cripps, speaking at Edinburgh on 15 February, likewise denied explicitly that fair shares meant equal shares. As reported in the *Glasgow Herald*, 'he gave an assurance that the Socialist goal of "fair shares for all" did not mean an equalitarian society in which everybody was exactly the same; it meant what it said.' But what *does* it say? Is the meaning of 'fair' so obvious that no explanation is needed? If Mr. Churchill, a master of the English language, was misled, it is not surprising that ordinary citizens were puzzled. The Glasgow *Evening Citizen* ran a 'Heckle Here' column, in which electors were invited to submit written questions to candidates. In the issue of 22 February, a constituent of Kelvingrove asked the Labour candidate to 'define the "fair shares for all" as advocated by Mr. Attlee and Sir Stafford Cripps as part of the Socialist policy'. The answer given was: 'See St. Mark, vi, 38–42. These verses are up-to-date and a permanent rule of life.' The verses in question recount the division of the loaves and fishes. The questioner might well wonder whether Labour policy was supposed to depend on miracles, or whether the point was after all that the loaves and fishes were equally divided. But presumably the candidate meant simply that food was to be made available to all. For most Labour election addresses treated 'fair shares' as meaning 'fair shares of food' ensured by the system of rationing. A number of addresses said: '*Fair Shares*. To secure food supplies in a situation of world scarcity, bulk buying was adopted. This ensures a fair supply for the nation; rationing ensures a fair supply for the individual, and subsidies and price control, which keep down prices, assist everyone to buy their share.' The booklet *Fifty Facts for Labour* says: 'The controlled distribution of food so that everybody gets a fair share is due to a Labour Government that believes the first job of the State is to see that the people are properly fed, irrespective of incomes or social status.'

But presumably the doctrine of fair shares extends beyond food. The Labour manifesto, and a number of Glasgow Labour election addresses, referred to the policy briefly as one of 'fair shares of life's necessities'. Man does not live by bread alone, and the necessities of life are not confined to food. Shelter, clothing, warmth, and a decent standard of health, are surely necessities of life, even at the basic material level. Most people nowadays would also think that such things as a reasonable measure of education are not frills but necessities. The fact is that 'fair shares of life's necessities' should cover the whole field of social security, a fair share for all of protection against a list of things like Lord Beveridge's 'five giants' of Want, Idleness, Squalor, Ignorance, and Disease. 'Fair shares of life's necessities' means a share for all of the basic necessities dealt with in 'the Beveridge programme', the philosophy underlying the Beveridge Report, which went beyond social insurance. It is the policy of the Welfare State. The Labour candidate for Cathcart made the Welfare State the main issue of his election address: 'Under Labour You Fare Well With Welfare. Under Tories It's Farewell To Welfare.'

In fact, however, all parties were committed to social security. There was a striking passage in the Conservative manifesto, *This is the Road*, perhaps due to Mr. Churchill himself, for he returned to it, as the hub of his policy, in national speeches and in messages to candidates, while the candidates themselves with very few exceptions, in Glasgow at least, ignored it—either because they did not understand its importance or possibly because Conservatism is by definition cautious with innovations. 'We are determined to give a solid base of social security below which none shall fall and above which each must be encouraged to rise to the utmost limit of his ability.' The first half of this sentence strikes a new note in Conservative policy. This was the answer to the charge that Conservatism is the doctrine of each for himself and devil take the hindmost. In this new Conservative policy, the weakest do not go to the wall. The wall is now to be cushioned with 'a solid base of social security below which none shall fall'. This 'solid base' is the same as the share of 'life's necessities' which Labour wishes to secure for all. But neither side seems to have understood that they were in agreement on this fundamental issue of social philo-sophy. They both held that irrespective of capacity and effort, *everyone* was to have the 'solid base' of a 'share in life's necessities'. *'None* shall fall' below this line, proclaims the Conservative mani-festo, not even 'the laggards' for whom Socialism was said to 'make life too easy'. The cushion was to be solid, not soft, but it was nevertheless to give some support to the laggard. Freedom for individual effort and ability, and the consequent inequalities of reward, were to have their scope only *above* this basic level of social security. Above this line 'each must be encouraged to rise to the utmost limit of his ability. We shall encourage instead of penalizing those who wish to create from their own efforts more security for themselves and their families.' Mr. Churchill, in a letter dated 3 February to local electors on behalf of Conservative candidates, repeated this conception as the essence of the Con-servative policy. 'The choice is simple. It is between a further plunge into socialism . . . or the adoption of the Unionist (and National Liberal) policy of a basic standard coupled with free opportunity for every individual to rise by the exercise of his own skill and qualities.' But the 'basic standard' was not an issue. Labour had always stood for that. Now that the Conservatives had adopted it too, it was common ground. Both sides were in agree-ment on the doctrine of a basic level or a share of life's necessities for all. They failed to perceive their agreement because they used different language and each barely understood its own slogan— let alone that of its opponents. 'They raised a dust, and then com-plained they could not see.'

Did the issue lie, then, in the question whether or not there was to be freedom, *above* the basic standard, for individuals to receive the unequal rewards of their unequal qualities and efforts? If so, why should a Labour candidate justify a high salary for a post requiring exceptional qualities and responsibility on the ground that fair shares did not mean equal shares? At the basic standard, the shares *are* roughly equal. 'Fair shares of food' under rationing means the *same* amount of butter, bacon, etc., for each person. It is a fair distribution because none goes without, but it is also an equal distribution. But when Mr. Churchill objected to the Labour policy of fair shares on the ground that it meant equal shares, he could not possibly have been objecting to the equal rationing of necessary commodities in short supply. He meant equal shares above the basic level, equal incomes for the whole of men's purchases, and he objected to that. Sir Stafford Cripps and other Labour spokesmen, however, emphatically rejected this interpretation of an equalitarian society. Fair shares did not mean eqaul shares. Nor does it. But the Labour spokesmen failed to say what it does mean. Fairness includes fair reward, reward proportionate to effort. It is unfair for the industrious to receive the same return as idlers. If fairness, then, includes just, but unequal, reward for unequal effort—includes, that is, the 'freedom to earn more by extra effort', while ensuring by its 'solid base' of 'life's necessities' for all that none shall have 'freedom to starve'—where is the conflict between the two philosophies? They both agree that there must be an equal basic standard for all, and freedom to pursue unequal rewards, in accordance with merit, above that standard. The conflict does not lie in the denial of either of these two elements by one party, but in the relative emphasis placed upon them. Labour stresses the basic standard, Conservatism stresses the freedom to rise high above it. In the words of the Conservative candidate for Gorbals, ambition is to be 'tempered' with a sense of responsibility to others; individual ambition comes first, social responsibility second. Labour would reverse the order of importance; 'fair shares' puts the cushion of the Welfare State first, and scope for individual initiative second.

Where do the Liberals stand in all this? They stand becalmed, the wind having been taken out of their sails by Conservatism on the one side and Labour on the other. Liberty is a Liberal idea. The name of the Liberal Party proclaims it, and it was a Liberal thinker, John Stuart Mill, who gave the classic political expression to the idea of Liberty as scope for the development of the individual according to his own desires and abilities. A Liberal was also the architect of the Welfare State with its buttresses of life's necessities for all against the 'giants' of want, idleness, squalor, ignorance, and disease. If 'fair shares for all' really means 'the Beveridge programme', the Liberal Party might well complain that the other two parties had filched the shining points of their philosophical spears from the Liberal armoury. However, there it is. In the great social issue of the election, the two main parties failed to see that they were quarrelling about emphasis, not about policies, that the two concepts of freedom and justice are complementary and not opposed, while the Liberal Party, whose thinkers have fitted the two together for the practical work of government, appeared to stand empty-handed because it could not take sides in a sham fight. But the impotence of the Liberal Party on the social issue was not wholly due to others. Although the issue between Conservatives and Socialists was misunderstood, an issue is there. It is not whether we should choose freedom or justice, for we must choose both, but which of the two we should emphasize the more. On this point, Liberals are divided among themselves. The older type of Liberal stresses individual liberty, as the Conservative does. The radical Liberal puts first, as Labour does, the Beveridge programme of social justice. On the whole, the former type of Liberalism stood out in the Liberal election policy as presented in Glasgow. Liberals indulged in scathing attacks on both the Conservative record and the Socialist policy of State monopoly, but the over-all impression given by their propaganda is that they stood a little Right of the centre. However, since in general social policy they tended to attack both sides instead of showing the complementary nature of the two philosophies, the Liberal approach seemed negative. Despite their claim that they alone gave electors something to vote *for*, while the other two parties simply showed things to vote *against*, the positive nature of their programme, on general social issues, failed to reveal itself. Their positive reforms of detail were all very well, but the effect of their argument in general went quite contrary to their intention. It became: 'You should vote *against* the Conservatives and *against* the Socialists. If you are *against* these two extremes, only we remain.' For all their desire to be positive, the Liberal appeal came over as negative. This was because they failed to show with sufficient clearness that their social philosophy is not the middle-road negation of two opposites but the combination of two complementaries.

In one respect, however, the Liberals did claim to be comprehensive where the two main parties were partial in their outlook. They claimed that the Conservative and Labour Parties each represented only one class of the community. Indeed, for all the honest endeavours of those two parties to avoid a sectional outlook, there is no doubt that on the whole the appeal of each gives the appearance of a class appeal. Of course, a member of the middle or higher-income group may respond to an emphasis placed on the needs of the poorer sections of the community, feeling that the greatest needs should be emphasized. Conversely, a Trade Unionist may respond to the appeal for freedom from governmental control. But such allegiances are few compared with the general run of response to class appeal. People living in a residential district take it for granted that most of their neighbours are Conservatives like themselves, and are a little surprised when they find that some, although having a similar income and business or professional background to their own, support Labour. When the newspapers pointed out that the Conservative candidate for Shettleston was an employee of the nationalized British Railways, the news-value of the information showed it to be an exception that proves the rule. Although Labour candidates addressing a predominantly professional audience might, in all sincerity, stress the ethical element of Socialism, some of their colleagues in working-class districts were prepared to appeal to class prejudice. On the Conservative side, talk of 'jobs for the boys' expressed class hostility no less. All this is doubtless the result of history, but whatever the causes, it is there. The Liberals claimed that they were the one party representing *all* the people, standing for the interests of the consumer. Yet much of their programme seemed designed especially from the viewpoint of the middle-income group. A member of the audience at a Liberal meeting got up after the speech of the candidate and said that the Liberals would receive more votes if they concentrated on Purchase Tax rather than Income Tax, as the latter did not greatly affect the average family man. The fact is that the Liberal policy did not make much appeal to 'the average family man'. Here, too, the Liberals failed in their effort to be comprehensive, and their policy was likely to catch the eye only of the 'in-betweens', leaving unaffected the two large groups normally attracted to vote Conservative and Labour respectively.

A word must be said of the 'also-rans'. Both the Communists and the I.L.P. accused Labour of failure and inability to pursue the path of Socialism. But the vast majority of the supporters of Socialism were unconvinced by the allegation that in remembering the fleshpots of Mr. Strachey they were forsaking the Law of Keir Hardie. To them Labour was Socialism enough. To non-Socialists it was more than enough.

3 Justice and Liberty

Some time ago, a series of B.B.C. programmes on the concept of
liberty began with a symposium to which Richard Crossman was
a contributor. The chairman of the symposium introduced Crossman as 'a Platonist', a strange description for the author of *Plato
To-day* (unless 'Platonist' was to mean a scholar rather than a
follower of Platonic doctrine). In the course of the symposium on
liberty, Crossman argued that the Liberal ideas of the nineteenth
century meant inordinate liberty for a few and precious little for the
majority; Socialism, he went on, restricted the economic liberty of
capitalists in order to spread liberty more widely in society. At the
end of the discussion the chairman said again that Crossman was a
Platonist, since he had been talking of justice and not liberty. That
Crossman was talking of justice is clear. That he was not talking of
liberty is less clear. To say that his emphasis on justice turned him
into a Platonist is absurd. In the *Republic*, Plato makes no bones of
his opposition to liberty. He opposes it in the name of *dikaiosyne*,
which I suppose he does intend his readers to understand as
'justice'. But whatever be the merits of his idea that every man
should be made to stick to his appointed job, it is plainly not what
we understand by justice, nor, I think, is it what most Athenians
would have understood by justice. Plato knew well enough that
whereas the prevailing ethos of an aristocratic society lies in each
man having his appointed station (the idea for which he appro-
priates the name of *dikaiosyne*),[1] the corresponding ethos of a democratic society is liberty; and Aristotle links the two concepts of
justice and liberty in democratic thought when he says, in Book V
of the *Nicomachean Ethics*, that aristocrats make the claims of
justice depend on excellence while democrats make them depend
on freedom.

Plato and Aristotle seem to have realized, then, that for democrats justice and liberty go together. It is often suggested, however,

that the principle (or alleged principle) of justice which is specially stressed by democratic thought, namely the principle of equality, is opposed to liberty. The opposition is emphasized—to take two familiar examples—in de Tocqueville's *Democracy in America* and in Mill's essay *On Liberty*. De Tocqueville indeed virtually identifies the idea of equality with that of 'democracy', and this equation is frequently taken for granted in countries with a shorter history than ours. The American professor, G. H. Sabine, in his *History of Political Theory*,[2] says that Mill's essay 'was in a sense a defense of liberty against democracy'. New Zealand students, when confronted with this quotation, do not seem to find at all paradoxical, as British politicians would, the implied opposition between liberty and democracy. But some British politicians would be ready to accept the antithesis if 'democracy' were replaced by 'equality'. In the General Election of 1950, Mr. Churchill was at pains to prove that the Socialists' slogan of 'fair shares for all' (which, of course, represented their emphasis on justice) meant equal shares. By contrast, the Conservative policy, as outlined by Mr. Churchill in a letter to electors on behalf of Conservative candidates, included 'free opportunity for every individual to rise by the exercise of his own skill and qualities'. The Socialists, for their part, seemed unwilling to have the principle of equal shares foisted upon them. Sir Stafford Cripps, replying to Mr. Churchill, 'gave an assurance that the Socialist goal of "fair shares for all" did not mean an equalitarian society in which everybody was exactly the same; it meant what it said'. But there were different views of what it did say. Some Labour literature interpreted the slogan as 'fair shares of food' under the rationing system. Other party literature described the policy as 'fair shares of life's necessities'. In discussing this matter elsewhere[3] I have suggested that, though the spokesmen of the Labour Party did not seem to realize it, 'fair shares of life's necessities' really meant social security or the Welfare State, a share for all of protection against Lord Beveridge's 'giants' of want, idleness, squalor, ignorance, and disease.

The policy of social security is, of course, endorsed by all the political parties of Britain. Conservatives and Liberals would not allow that it is a Socialist prerogative. Now in this scheme, the benefits provided *are* based on a principle of equality. Under rationing everybody is entitled to an equal share of butter and bacon. Certain classes of people with special needs are entitled to more, but we shall see later that distribution according to need depends likewise on the claim of equality. Again, under social insurance everyone who is unable to work by reason of old age, unemployment, or sickness, receives the same amount of money. The Welfare State is not, however, 'an equalitarian society in which everybody is exactly the same', because its equalitarianism is confined to basic necessities. The Conservative manifesto for the General Election accused Socialism of denying 'enterprise its reward while making life too easy for the laggards'. But the rewards of enterprise, Conservatives would have to agree, should apply only after basic necessities have been provided for all, the enterprising and the laggards alike. For elsewhere the Conservative manifesto stated: 'We are determined to give a solid base of social security below which none shall fall and above which each must be encouraged to rise to the utmost limit of his ability.' There was, then, no opposition between freedom and equality in the policies advocated by both parties; all were to be ensured an equal share of life's necessities, irrespective of ability or enterprise, while the winning of 'rewards' over and above basic necessities was left to the freedom of the individual. In current social policy, at least one aspect of freedom is related to one aspect of a principle of justice, that of desert, the rewards of merit, and this freedom is not held (despite the confusions of political utterance) to clash with an application of the principle of equality. In this essay I wish to examine more closely the part played, in modern democratic thought, by these two principles of social justice, and to consider their relation to the concept of liberty.

ii

The notion of justice has traditionally been divided into (a) distributive and (b) retributive or corrective justice. (I do not propose to discuss 'commutative justice', which prescribes a fair exchange in contracts. The demand here is that the goods or services to be exchanged should be deemed of equal value, and the rating of such 'value' is an economic question.) I take distributive justice to refer to a principle of equality in some sense. The difficulty is to specify that sense. Retributive or corrective justice I take to refer to the claims of reparation and of desert. 'Reparation' here is used in a wider sense than the normal, to mean both the making good of injury (the ordinary sense of 'reparation') and the readiness to requite benefits that is implied in the obligation of gratitude. 'Desert' refers primarily to the merit of virtue and the demerit of vice, in consequence of which the first is thought to call for reward and the second for punishment; the ideas of 'merit' and 'reward' (but rarely, in a converse sense, those of 'demerit' and 'punishment') are also extended to express the praise accorded to certain non-moral qualities and activities and to the benefits that are accordingly regarded as their due. I have distinguished reparation from desert only in order to ignore the former in what follows. For social theory, and in particular for the relation of justice to liberty, the principles of justice that are relevant are those of equality and desert.

Theorists who deny or ignore the alleged claim to equality sometimes treat the claim of desert, i.e. the apportionment of happiness or the means to it in accordance with merit (or perhaps merit and capacity), as *distributive* justice, since such apportionment is, in their view, the one proper principle of distribution. Sir David Ross,[4] for example, uses the word 'justice' to refer to the distribution of happiness in accordance with desert, and evidently does not recognize any claim to equality other than the 'proportionate equality' which Aristotle declares such distribution to be. The word 'retribution' may then be used to refer solely to one way, not necessarily the right way, of looking at punishment. Since I shall argue that there is, in the moral thinking of our society at least, a claim to equality other than the so-called 'proportionate equality', I retain the name of distributive justice for the claim to equality, and I subsume the requital of desert, whether by way of reward or by way of punishment, under retributive justice.[5] If this diversity of usage is confusing, we may speak simply of the alleged principle or claim of equality and the alleged principle or claim of desert. By a 'moral claim' I mean nothing other than a moral obligation, considered as *what* is owed to the person or persons towards whom the obligation is felt.

I have spoken, for the moment, of *alleged* principles of equality and desert, because it may be denied that either of them is a moral principle standing on its own. As we have seen, it may be denied that there is any valid claim to equality, except where distribution according to desert requires, as a special case, equal distribution to those of equal desert. Moralists who take what is often called a 'deontological' view of the standard of right, generally agree that the principle of desert is a cardinal, if not the sole, element in justice and that this is different from, and may conflict with, considerations of social utility. Some of them, for example Richard Price and Sir David Ross, do not recognize as an additional element of justice any claim to equality. Conversely, the hedonistic utilitarians regarded the idea of desert as falling under the claim of utility, while (in their unconfused moods) they felt bound to posit a principle of equality separate from the obligation to promote general happiness as such.

I propose to consider first, whether the concept of merit can be reduced to that of social utility; and secondly, whether there is a positive claim to equality, and if so, in what sense. I shall argue that neither desert nor equality can be wholly reduced to considerations of social utility or absolutely rejected as valid moral claims. I shall maintain that both are, to a degree, independent moral claims in modern democratic thought, that they are correctly subsumed under the one concept of justice as being alike protections of the interests of the individual, and as such, they are, I shall argue, not fundamentally different from the thought that is basic to the idea of liberty.

iii

According to the principle of desert, it is held that virtue merits reward and vice punishment. Does this mean that the virtuous man ought to receive reward, and the vicious punishment, i.e. that someone ought to give them what they are said to deserve? Difficulty arises with ill-desert. If a man has deliberately done wrong when he could have done right, we say he deserves punishment, but does this mean or imply in every case that someone ought to punish him? The trend of modern opinion is that the actual infliction of punishment is to be justified only if it will lead to a balance of good, that it is to be justified by utilitarian considerations of deterrence and reform. Where there is an obligation to punish, therefore, the obligation seems to depend, at least in part, on the future consequences of the act. But desert clearly depends not on the future but on the past. The statement that a man deserves punishment is justified by the fact that he *has* deliberately and knowingly acted contrary to what he saw to be his duty. To say that he deserves punishment, then, cannot mean the same as saying that someone ought to punish him, for the two statements differ in their implications. The first implies that he has acted contrary to thought of duty, and implies nothing about future consequences. The second implies that the punishment will have good consequences, though it also implies that the man deserves to be punished. The second includes the first but also goes beyond it.

Utilitarians attempt to cut this knot in the following way. They hold that punishment is justified solely by its consequences. The idea of ill-desert, included in that of punishment, is a concealed way of referring to, and achieving, good consequences. According to the utilitarian account of punishment, '*A* deserves punishment' means: (1) '*A* has done an act of a type that is harmful to the public and that tends to be prevented by punishment or the threat of it.' (2) 'Therefore, it will be useful to punish him.' The word 'punishment' here simply means the infliction of pain, with the promise of its repetition, in circumstances where a socially harmful tendency manifests itself and is of such a nature that fear of pain can cause the suppression or inhibition of future manifestations. When we say that the punishment 'fits' the crime, we are referring, not to any specifically ethical relation between them, but simply to the causal property which the punishment has of tending to remove or repress the harmful tendency. A similar account, *mutatis mutandis*, would be given of meriting reward. (A forceful modern statement of this theory of punishment and reward is given by Professor P. H. Nowell-Smith in an article, 'Freewill and Moral Responsibility', published in *Mind*, January 1948.)

The objections to this account are twofold. (1) Punishment and reward are not the sole type of action (or indeed of painful and pleasurable action) that is useful in averting public harm or promoting public good. Quarantine is useful in averting public harm, and it happens to involve, as imprisonment designedly includes, the experience of isolation, which to most people is unpleasant. Instruction makes people useful to society, and to some it is pleasant (and so like reward), to others painful (and so like punishment).

Taking medicine benefits society as well as the patient, since a sick person is a burden on society; and it may be unpleasant. Yet it is not called punishment. Sermons are intended to strengthen our morality, to reinforce our virtue and to correct our vice; the virtuous may perhaps find them gratifying, and the vicious may find them tedious. Are we to say that sermons are rewards to the one and punishments to the other? These are, of course, the stock objections to the simpler utilitarian theories of punishment, that they would assimilate to punishment all prevention of social harm and all reform. The more elaborate utilitarian theory outlined above would avoid calling some (though not all) of our examples by the name of punishment, since it recognizes that punishment differs from other types of deterrence and reform in looking to guilt and consequent ill-desert. But it gives a secondary utilitarian account of 'guilt' and 'desert', which is open to a similar sort of criticism, namely that it is too wide. This defect of the utilitarian analysis of desert constitutes our second objection.

(2) On the utilitarian theory of desert, we should have to say, where any action causes the removal of an undesirable tendency or the strengthening of a desirable one, not only that the action is to be called punishment or reward, but that the person to whom it is directed 'deserves' it, since the propriety or fittingness of desert simply expresses this causal relation, in the same sense in which medicine is appropriate for the cure of sickness. Indeed, the sick person 'deserves' his medicine. The donkey deserves his blows or carrots, and his laziness or energy are to be called immoral or moral. We do not in fact use the language of morality in such circumstances. When we speak of desert we imply that the agent knew what he was doing, could control his action at that time, and was aware of a right and a wrong. We say that punishment is justified when it is *both* useful *and* deserved.

I agree with the utilitarian theory of punishment to the extent of thinking that where there is an obligation to punish, the obligation arises from utility. The strength of the so-called retributive (or, as I prefer to call it, the desert) theory of punishment lies, not in the justification of a positive obligation to punish the guilty, but in the protection of innocence. The utilitarian theory, taken alone, requires us to say, with Samuel Butler's Erewhonians, that sickness is a crime which deserves the punishment of medicine. It also requires us to say, when 'it is expedient that one man should die for the people', that he deserves this as a punishment. It is here that common sense protests against the 'injustice' of utilitarianism, and it is here that the 'retributive' theory of punishment has greatest force. Punishment is permissible only if it is deserved. But this does not of itself give rise to an obligation to punish. An obligation to inflict punishment, where punishment is permitted by desert, arises from the social utility of its infliction. Where there is no guilt, the infliction of pain on a particular person may still be socially useful, but the claim of social utility is opposed by the claim of the individual to be treated as an 'end-in-himself' and not merely as a means to the ends of society. Where, however, a person is guilty of having wilfully done wrong, he has thereby forfeited part of his claim to be treated as an end-in-himself; in acting as a non-moral being he leaves it open to his fellows to use him as such.[6] Such forfeit of his claim not to be pained does not of itself give rise to an obligation to pain him, for his ill-desert consists in the removal, not the creation, of a claim with its corresponding obligation. The guilt does not constitute, or give rise to, a claim on the part of the guilty person to be punished, i.e. an obligation on the part of others to punish him. It removes, to the degree to which he has infringed another's rights, his normal claim not to be pained, i.e. it removes, to that degree, the obligation of others not to pain him. Where there is a positive obligation to punish him, this is the obligation to the public at large to safeguard their security, and the corresponding claim is the claim of the public to have their security safeguarded.

This obligation to, or claim of, the public at large exists, of course, at all times, and if the fulfilment of it involves pain for an innocent individual it still has its force. But the claim of the public in such circumstances conflicts with the claim of the individual not to be pained, to be treated as an end, and sometimes the one claim, sometimes the other, is thought to be paramount in the circumstances. If it should be thought necessary to override the claim of the individual for the sake of the claim of society, our decision is coloured by compunction, which we express by saying that the claim of justice has to give way to that of utility. Where the individual has been guilty of deliberate wrongdoing, however, his claim not to be pained is thought to be removed; there is held to be no conflict of claims now, no moral *obstat* raised by justice to the fulfilment of the claim of utility. This thought is expressed by saying that the individual 'deserves' his pain, and the pain is called 'punishment', which is simply a way of saying that in this situation the infliction of pain, for the sake of social utility, involves no trespass on the claims of justice, no conflict between utility and justice. Justice is 'satisfied' by the 'punishment', for justice has not, in the circumstances of guilt, a countervailing claim that would have been breached by pursuing the path of utility.

In giving this interpretation of the saying that 'justice is satisfied by punishment', I do not imply that the statement has always had the meaning which I am now attributing to it (or rather, recommending for it). Clearly it used to have a more positive meaning. No doubt it originally referred to the satisfaction of the desire for vengeance. My point is that our present moral thinking recoils, as opponents of the retributive theory rightly insist, from justifying punishment by mere retaliation, but at the same time it does give an important place to justice in the idea of punishment. This role of justice, I am suggesting, is the protection of innocence, the raising of a moral *obstat* to the infliction of pain on an innocent individual. Where we think that, despite the moral *obstat* of justice, the pain must be inflicted for the sake of utility, we recognize the claim of justice at least to the extent of using different language. It may be *expedient*, but not just, that one man should die for the people. 'Expediency' then has the a-moral or anti-moral connotation which it bears when 'expediency' is contrasted with 'principle'. But where the victim of expediency is guilty, he has forfeited the claim of justice; now we may speak of his pain as 'punishment', as 'deserved'. Expediency here does not conflict with 'principle', i.e. with justice, but is itself 'principle'. Not that the punishment is now *required* by justice. The 'principle' that requires the 'punishment' is the principle of safeguarding public security, i.e. expediency itself. Justice does not demand the punishment; justice stands aside, for it is satisfied that its claims raise no obstruction. Of course, expediency does not become 'principle' only when justice stands aside. The claim of social utility is always a valid claim. It is the claim of the members of society in general not to be harmed.

By contrasting the claim of justice, as looking to the interests of the individual, with the claim of utility, as looking to the interests of society at large, I do not imply that society is anything other

D

than its members. In our practical deliberations, however, we often find it convenient to think of 'the interests of society' as an abstracted entity, since we may know from experience that a course of action is likely to benefit or harm a number of members of our society while not knowing which particular members will be affected on this occasion. The dangers of the abstraction are countered by the concept of justice, which emphasizes the claims of the individual as such.

The idea of demerit, I have suggested, signifies the removal of a claim normally present. The idea of merit, of virtue deserving happiness, signifies the presence of an additional claim to those normally present. To say that virtue itself implies a claim to happiness (i.e. an obligation on the part of others to bestow happiness) does not give rise to the same difficulty as saying that vice itself implies an obligation on the part of others to punish it. A virtuous man would of course not claim any reward for his virtue, so that it seems odd to talk of there being a 'claim'. In normal usage the word 'claim' often suggests the idea of claiming on the part of the person said to have the claim. I use the word 'claim', however, as a term of art to express nothing more than the relation of obligation viewed as what is felt to be owed to the person towards whom the agent has the obligation. I should be glad to substitute a different word, if I could find one, that does not suggest the idea of a claim being *made* by the person who is described, in my usage, as 'having' a claim. When I say that the virtuous man has an additional claim by reason of his virtue, all I mean is that others have an additional obligation to him. The bestowal of further positive happiness upon a person already reasonably content (as opposed to the removal, or the non-infliction, of misery) is, in the general relations between man and man, usually thought to go beyond the requirements of strict obligation, to be the part of a supererogatory beneficence. But if a man has exhibited virtue, we feel (as also in certain situations of special relationship, e.g. between husband and wife, or parent and child) that the addition of further positive happiness is 'called for', that it comes within the sphere of our obligation. Good-desert, then, expresses the presence of an additional claim to the normal (i.e. the existence of an additional obligation on the part of other people towards the virtuous person said to be meritorious), while ill-desert expresses the absence of a normal claim (i.e. the removal of a normal obligation of others towards the person said to exhibit demerit). The obligation to reward virtue for its own sake is, however, not a strong one, if only because any thought on the part of the virtuous agent that his virtue merits reward is liable to make his motive to some degree interested and to that extent less virtuous. Rewards are usually conferred for the sake of utility, and the utilitarian account of reward covers even more of the truth than does its account of punishment. With punishment, the utilitarian account is deficient in failing to cover the protection of innocence, the claim of which often conflicts with and overrides that of public utility. The claim of virtue, however, usually coincides with that of utility, since the encouragement of virtue is socially useful, and therefore little compunction is felt in accepting the utilitarian justification of reward. If, in some exceptional cases, there is a conflict between the claim of virtue to reward and the claim of public utility, no one would deny that the claim of utility takes precedence. However, though the non-utilitarian claim of merit is slight, it is there, and when we say that the reward should be given not only *pour encourager les autres* but also because it is deserved, the use of the term 'desert' or 'merit' expresses the existence of an additional claim to the normal, as the use of 'demerit' or 'deserving punishment' expresses the absence of a normal claim.

The main force of retributive justice, then, lies in its assertion of the claim of the innocent individual to be treated as an end and not merely as a means to the general interest. Now when a man is said to have a right (in my language, a claim) to liberty, this means that other men are obliged not to interfere with his legitimate desires. The claim to liberty is the demand for moral protection of the individual's wishes provided these be not themselves contrary to any moral injunction. The claim of retributive justice that the individual who has not 'deserved ill' (i.e. who has not forfeited the protection of justice by wilful wrongdoing) be treated as an end, and his claim to liberty, are two aspects of a single moral claim. They are alternative ways of expressing the same moral demand, that an individual who has not deliberately contravened the requirements of morality be treated as an 'end-in-himself', with the stress on the negative element of not treating him as a means to the ends of others; the demand is that we leave him to pursue his natural ends and do not interfere by going against his desires. The claim of good-desert also requires the person concerned to be treated as an 'end', but with the stress on the positive obligation to 'make his ends our own', that is, to obtain for him the happiness that everyone naturally desires. This is of course different from the negative claim of liberty to be left alone.

So far, I have discussed the notion of desert as meaning *morally* deserving. We do, however, also use the concept of desert in a different way. We say that 'enterprise should receive its just reward', that 'genius deserves recognition', that 'the incompetent deserve to fail'. This sense of desert is made up of two notions; first, that certain capacities and activities are socially useful while other activities are socially harmful, and that the encouragement of the former and disparagement of the latter are socially useful; secondly, it also includes the idea that a man has a 'right' to reap the benefits or ill effects of his own activities. The latter idea suggests that a man has a 'right' to, or 'deserves', the natural consequences of the exercise of capacities or defects for the possession of which he is not *morally* deserving of praise or blame. I do not think it plays so important a part in our idea of non-moral desert as does the idea of social utility, but it undoubtedly does play a part. Looked at in one way, it does not express any ethical idea at all, but merely asserts what *are* the natural consequences of certain activities: 'whatsoever a man soweth, that shall he also reap'; 'the sins of the fathers shall be visited upon the children'; this is the way of the world. But an ethical connotation is liable to attach itself to the use of the expressions 'a right' and 'deserves', and even to the prophetic 'shall'. Such ethical connotation may or may not be justified. So far as evil consequences are concerned, to say that a man 'deserves' the results of his natural defects (e.g. of his ignorance, stupidity, or clumsiness), would generally be regarded, to the extent that the use of the word 'deserves' conveys an ethical connotation, as itself an *immoral* judgment. This would not be true if we thought that the extent of the defect was in part due to a failure to exercise effort at improvement; then the 'desert' would attach to that failure and not strictly to the defective capacity. Likewise, the ethical connotation of the statement that enterprise 'deserves' its 'reward' may in part express approval of the effort that has been involved. More prominent, however, is the idea that the 'rewards' of such activities are natural consequences which ought not to be interfered with. There would be little point in saying that a Robinson Crusoe 'deserved' the benefits of his ingenuity, for there was no one to propose interference with his enjoyment of them. Were a man solitary, it would be futile to say, in Hobbesian fashion, that he had a 'right' to such satisfactions as he could achieve. We assert his 'right' only when there is someone else who might propose to deny him the enjoyment of the natural consequences of his activity. In then asserting his 'right' (or claim) we assert an obligation on the part of others not to interfere, and this is again the claim of liberty. The 'just' rewards of enterprise depend in part on utility and in part on the idea of moral protection for the unhindered use by an individual of the advantageous capacities with which he has been endowed. Again the claim of justice and the claim of liberty coincide.

iv

I turn next to the principle of equality. Many people who would agree that the principle of desert may go hand in hand with the claims of liberty would deny that liberty is compatible with equality. The first difficulty is to decide whether there is any valid principle of equality. Nobody in his senses would say that the alleged claim to equality is a claim that all men *are* equal. The first of the 'truths' held 'to be self-evident' by the American Declaration of Independence is 'that all men are created equal'. Similarly the French Declaration of 1789 begins 'Men are born free and equal'. 'Rubbish,' retorts the realist who cannot recognize a metaphor when he sees one, 'Ivan Ivanovitch is born with poor physique, poor brains, poor parents, and as a slave of Mr. Stalin; Henry Ford junior is born with good physique, good brains, a millionaire father, and as a free citizen of the free-enterprise U.S.A.' Locke and Rousseau, the Pilgrim Fathers and the French Revolutionaries, the drafters and the signatories of the U.N.O. Declaration of Human Rights, all knew perfectly well that men are not born equal in endowments, possessions, or opportunities. What they and their declarations say is that men are equal in respect of their *rights*, i.e. that in some sense men have a claim to equality, not that they *are* equal.

It may be said that a claim to equality must depend on an

existing equality. If men have a claim to be considered or treated equally, this can only be because they are already equal in some respect which involves an obligation to treat them equally in action affecting them. It is often held that the claim to equality depends on religious doctrine and is an illustration of the fact that the whole of morality does. The ideals of liberty, equality, and fraternity, that have made themselves felt in western civilization since the French Revolution, owe their origin, it is claimed, to Christianity and rest on Christian doctrine. That they originated with the religious doctrine I think we may admit. Whether they can logically be derived from it is more dubious. The justification for equal treatment despite natural inequality, it is said, is the fact that, in religious doctrine, we are all the children of God and are therefore brothers. But does this metaphor help? It says that I should treat every man as I treat my brothers, i.e. as love would prompt, and wishes to persuade me that this is my duty by affirming that, morally and religiously though not biologically, all men arc my brothers; moral conduct towards other men, i.e. my duty to them, is therefore the same in content as my natural conduct to my natural brothers. But does a man always love each of his brothers *equally*? Or as much as he may love one or two of his friends, or his wife, or his children? His children—there, it might be said, is the point. God loves us all as his children, and he loves us equally. For if you ask a parent which of his children he loves best, he will tell you that he loves each of them equally. This is not always true; did not Jacob love Joseph best? But even if it is true, does it follow that because a father loves his children equally, they will love each other equally? No, it will be replied, but they *should*. The doctrine of the fatherhood of God and the consequent brotherhood of man, however, was meant to tell us *why* we should love each other equally. It was intended to do this by giving us reason to regard those who are not literally our brothers as if they were. But the use of the image does not necessarily convey with it the idea of equality. Where a group of people are literally of the same family, they may think that they *ought* to act with equal love to each of their brethren, but their kinship does not necessarily cause them to do so nor does it give them a reason why they ought to do so. A man may consider both that he has an obligation to treat his brothers equally and that he has an obligation to treat all men equally, but he may still ask why in *each* of the two cases. The fact that he and his brothers have a common parent who loves them equally seems irrelevant.

The religious doctrine so far considered, then, does not give a basis for the claim to equality. But perhaps we have not seized upon the crucial element in the doctrine. It may be argued that the principle of equality rests on the fact that all men are born equal as moral agents, as having the dignity of a moral being, i.e. of the capacity to be moral, and thus they are equal in the sight of God. Other theologians, I have been told, interpret 'equality in the sight of God' as equality in sin; we are all born equally steeped in original sin. Whether or not we accept the latter interpretation of 'equality in the sight of God', it is of course true that all men are potential moral agents and therefore have an equal 'dignity' not possessed by beings incapable of morality. But this equality is not what an enslaved or downtrodden populace refers to in claiming equality of rights. The 'rights' or claims of justice are claims to *happiness* (or the opportunity to pursue happiness, or the means to happiness). Nobody would say that the equality of all men as potential moral agents involves equal claims to happiness, and it is to be hoped that the upholders of original sin do not think that all men have equal claims to misery, that they are all *equally* damned. If we are to consider the relation between our *moral* natures and our claims to happiness, it seems more reasonable to say that moral achievement, not mere potentiality, is what counts in determining 'rights' or claims; the non-equalitarian principle of desert supplies the connecting link.

It is for this reason that some moralists would deny the validity of any positive claim to equality. If men are equal only in moral potentiality, and if claims to happiness are determined by moral achievement, in which men are unequal, how can we say they have equal claims? Accordingly, it may be held, the principle of desert is the sole principle of 'distributive justice' and there is no claim to equal distribution apart from this. 'Distributive justice', the argument would run, following Aristotle, is a distribution according to merit; unequal shares to unequals, and equal shares to equals. Equal distribution is right only when there is equal merit.

To sustain this view, we must interpret 'merit' widely, as at the end of Section iii. Inequality, whether of liberty, wealth, opportunity, or other desirable things, may be justified by differences of moral merit, of economic 'merit', or of natural 'merit'; a man who has wilfully committed a crime 'deserves' to be imprisoned; an enterprising manufacturer 'deserves' the fruits of his success; a bright child 'deserves' a good education. Taking 'merit' in this wide sense, it may be claimed that just distribution is always in accordance with merit.

What, then, are we to say of claims to equality? That these, when justified, are always based on equal merit? This suggestion would cover only a proportion of the relevant instances. It may be held, however, that claims to equality are usually to be interpreted negatively as justified protests against particular inequalities, justified not because there is any positive claim to equality but because the inequality is not 'deserved', i.e. has an improper ground. It is unjust that Aristides be selected for ostracism; that a businessman become rich by 'profiteering', that is, by making large profits in circumstances in which the general interest is harmed by his 'enterprise'; that a dull-witted Vere de Vere be selected for Eton in preference to a bright Smith. The ground of the particular inequality attacked is morally 'irrelevant', while an existing 'relevant' ground for differentiation is ignored. The objection is not to inequality as such but to the ground of differentiation. The unequal treatment has conflicted with merit, where 'merit' can mean moral worth, social utility, or natural capacity. In these respects men are of unequal 'worth', and their treatment or status, it may be held, should be in accordance with their different 'worths'. But throughout history unequal treatment has almost always far exceeded, or cut across, the differences of 'worth'. Some men are of lesser 'worth' than others, but none are so much less valuable than others that they should be their serfs, still less their slaves or chattels. Even where those treated as of less account have not been serfs but just a lower class, the higher class has seldom consisted of those who are more 'worthy' in virtue, utility, or capacity; usually, membership of the privileged class has been based on birth or similar accidents. Accordingly, the argument might conclude, the cry for equality is really a cry against unjustified inequality; but if, *per impossibile*, human affairs could be so arranged that men were treated in accordance with their natural inequalities, all would be well. To treat them equally, however, when they are naturally unequal, is just as wrong as to exaggerate or to run directly counter to their natural inequalities.

This view of course smacks of the 'aristocrat', the 'superior person', and therefore in these days many of us have a prejudice against it. But it cannot be easily dismissed, and the difficulty of justifying a positive claim to equality in the face of natural inequality tempts one to think that it must be true. Further, it need not in practice lead to aristocracy, for a modern exponent of the theory may agree that if, like Plato, we try to adjust our human affairs to the degree of inequality conferred on men by nature, we shall be sure to make a mess of it. The advice that the theory might offer for practice is this: 'We should neither try to secure equality nor try to adjust treatment to nature. Both are impracticable. What we should do, and what successful reformers have in fact done, is to protest against and remove unjustified inequality, inequality that clearly goes against the inequalities of nature. If we stick to this task, we shall have plenty to do, and shall not be led into extravagant and impracticable paths.'

As practical advice, I think this is sensible; and the view does contain a great part of the truth about equality. Where the cry for equality has reference to the claims of 'worth', i.e. of moral merit, natural capacity, or social utility, it is not based on a positive belief in equality but is a negative plea against unjustified inequality. To this extent the claim to equality is negative.

But the theory, as expounded so far, omits one of the justifying grounds for unequal treatment, and this ground, paradoxical though it appears at first sight, points to a limited positive claim to equality. Unequal treatment may be justified, not only on account of the different 'worths' of the recipients, but also on account of their different needs. We think it right to make special provision for those affected by special needs, through natural disability, such as mental or physical weakness, or through the slings and arrows of outrageous fortune, through sickness, unemployment, or destitute old age. Here, it would seem, we go *against* nature, and think ourselves justified in doing so. The unequal treatment meted out is in *inverse* proportion to natural inequalities. We attempt to remedy, so far as we can, the inequality of nature. Though in the mere provision of aid, monetary or other, we seem at first sight to do more for the needy person than for the normal, to make an unequal discrimination in favour of the former, the inequality of treatment is an attempt to reduce the existing inequality, to bring the needy person up to the same level of advantages as the normal. We try to make up for the natural inequality and to give the handicapped, so far as possible, equal opportunities and equal satisfactions to those possessed by the non-handicapped.

It is, however, an exaggeration to say, without qualification, that justice here is a matter of going against nature. For in dealing with the handicaps with which some people are born, we usually cannot provide them with fully equal opportunities to those possessed by normal people. We can try, as the theory we are considering bids us, to see that their handicap is not allowed, by the social arrangements of man, to extend beyond what it naturally must be. In the past, for example, handicapped children were neglected while normal children were, for reasons of utility, given opportunity for development. We think that we ought to remedy the neglect, to give the handicapped child such opportunities for development as his natural capacities allow. We try to ensure that the inequalities of nature are not exaggerated, but we cannot remove the natural inequalities themselves.

Yet it would be a mistake to think that, because some natural handicaps cannot be removed, there is no obligation to remove those which we can. If we can cure congenital blindness, we think we have an obligation to do so. We do not think that illness should simply be left to take its natural course; sometimes 'leaving it to nature' is the best way to cure illness, sometimes not, and we think we ought to take the course, natural or not, which will be most likely to effect the cure. Where a person's peculiar disadvantages are due to external causes, such as an economic slump, an earthquake, or a flood, we certainly think that we should remedy them and, if possible, prevent them.

The claim of need, then, involves a distribution not in accordance with existing differences but contrary to them. People do of course differ in their needs, so that the provision of satisfaction for them will be an unequal one. But strictly, the potential needs and desires of people, even the most fortunate, are unlimited. Although I have not the special need of an invalid for eggs, I could do with quite a lot. Although normal children do not have the special need of the handicapped child for special educational equipment and personal supervision, they could quite well do with better educational equipment and more personal supervision than they now receive. How do we determine when a need is a 'special' need? Our recognition of 'special' needs is a recognition that some persons, by reasons of nature or accident, fall below the normal level of satisfactions, below the level which most people enjoy and which we regard as essential for decent living. Our attempt to meet these special needs is an attempt to bring such people up to the normal level of satisfactions, or as near to it as we can. When we do more for the handicapped child or the disabled man, this is a recognition that they are at present unequal to (below) most people in capacity to earn their living and have a reasonably happy life. Our unequal (greater) provision of care for them is an attempt to reduce the existing inequality; we want, so far as we can, to bring them to a level of equality with others in capacity to enjoy their lives. Thus the basis of the claim of special need is really a recognition of a claim to equality. It is a positive moral claim taking its place with others such as the claims of moral worth, utility, and capacity. For note that this claim of need remains even if there is no other moral claim. The permanently disabled, the aged, the insane, have, we think, a claim to be taken care of, to a reasonable measure of comfort and happiness, even though they are incapable of making any return.

V

Having established that there is a positive claim to equality, let us now consider more directly its content. To what precisely do we regard people as having an equal claim? Equality of what? Of consideration, of opportunity, of material goods, or of happiness? Certainly to equality of consideration; i.e. we recognize the right of *everyone* to have his various claims considered. But this is only a way of saying that everyone *has* claims; it does not involve any additional content as the claim of distributive justice. We also recognize a claim to equality of opportunity, that is, a claim of every man to an equal chance of developing his capacities and pursuing his interests. Is there also a claim to equal distribution? That is, when material means to happiness are available, should they, in the absence of other claims, be distributed equally? The question may be put alternatively thus: have men a claim to equal happiness, or only to an equal chance of pursuing happiness? In fact, of course, equal happiness cannot be secured. If, for instance, everyone were given the same amount of money, the different tastes of different persons, and the different costs of satisfying their tastes, would mean that the same amount of money would provide more happiness for some than for others; if I like beer and you like whisky, I should be able to say 'Nunc est bibendum' more often than you. Again, some would, by luck or greater ability, soon turn their standard income into a larger one, while others would soon be paupers. However, this practical impossibility of providing equal happiness does not affect the theoretical question. For many obligations cannot in practice be fully satisfied. If, for example, it be held that we have an obligation to increase the sum of happiness or good, or to distribute happiness in accordance with merit, this is in practice often impossible. The relevant obligation is really to try to aim at or approach the proposed ideal.

Let us first see what is involved in 'equality of opportunity'. I think that this is bound up with the idea of liberty. The idea of liberty is, primarily, a negative one, the removal of restraints upon doing what one wishes. Such restraints may be imposed by the actions of other persons or may be due to natural obstacles. Social liberty refers to the removal of restraints by other persons. The restraints of nature may be external or internal. The Firth of Clyde prevents me from walking to Bute, and if I wish to get to Bute a ferry must be provided. But besides such external obstacles to the satisfaction of our desires, there are also internal restraints. If I want to be a champion tennis-player, I am restrained by the weakness of my sight. Of internal restraints, some can be removed, others cannot. I have not the natural endowment to become a good tennis-player, but I have the natural endowment to become a fair chess-player. Natural endowments, however, cannot always be exercised by their possessor without training and suitable environment; in the absence of these, they remain unfulfilled potentialities. My potential capacity to become a fair chess-player is subject to the natural restraint that, if left to itself without training and practice, it cannot be actualized. Suitable training and practice are the removal of the natural restraint on the exercise of natural potentialities. Two children may have the potentiality of becoming good craftsmen. If one is given the necessary training and suitable environment to enable him to develop his potentialities so as to lead a satisfying life and to be socially useful, he thereby receives opportunity to make the most of his capacities. If the other is not given such training, he is denied the opportunity to make the most of his capacities. Equal opportunity means, ideally, maximum opportunity for all to develop the potentialities they have, and failing that, the maximum that is possible in the face of, e.g., economic difficulties. The opportunity is to be equally, i.e. impartially, spread in the sense that discrimination in the provision of a particular type of opportunity for some and not for others should depend on the potentialities that the prospective recipients have, instead of depending on 'irrelevant' considerations such as birth or wealth.

Social liberty, we said, is the absence of restraint by other persons. The provision of opportunity, however, involves, not the absence of action by other persons, but its presence in the form of aid and training in the development of capacities. Liberal political philosophy concentrated on social liberty. But the mere absence of interference by others does not give full opportunities to all to pursue happiness in accordance with their capacities, because many capacities do not develop of themselves but need assistance. When J. S. Mill rests the claim to liberty on the value of 'the development of individuality', he implies an extension of the old Liberal idea of liberty. It would be generally agreed by thoughtful people today that men have a moral claim not only to social liberty but also to liberty in the further sense of maximum development of potentiality. Equal liberty for all will not result in equal happiness, for men differ in their potentialities so that some will be more able than others to achieve happiness for themselves by the exercise of their developed capacities.

Let us now turn to the other suggested principle of equal satisfactions. There seems to be some claim that all should be given equal satisfactions to the extent that this is within our power, e.g. in the provision of material means to happiness. This principle would conflict with the principle of maximum opportunity for all, if the latter were taken to imply not only that a man should be enabled to develop his potentialities to the fullest extent but also that he should be allowed to use his developed capacities as he wishes for his own maximum enjoyment. The second of these two implications is required by the principle of social liberty, and the two together by a combination of the principle of maximum opportunity with the principle of social liberty. The principle of opportunity alone, however, need not necessarily be held to conflict with the principle of equal satisfactions, for a man might be enabled to develop his capacities but required to devote the fruits of his capacities to the common good; that is to say, he might be expected to retain or receive, for his own enjoyment, a roughly equal amount of material means to satisfaction as others, while any surplus material results of his exercise of capacity were distributed to others whose own capacities did not allow them to effect as much. This is the equalitarian position—from each according to his capacity, to each according to his needs. The position conflicts with the principle of maximum social liberty, but not with the principle of maximum opportunity.

In practice, however, neither the position of extreme Liberalism nor the position of extreme equalitarianism is acceptable in isolation. The equalitarian has to give some weight to social liberty for the sake of utility, that is, in order to provide incentives to production so that the needs which can be satisfied may be at a maximum. There is in fact no limit to the desires which can be satisfied, so that distribution 'to each according to his needs' must always be below what could be done. Accordingly, certain desires, which are thought to be more fundamental than others, are distinguished by the name of 'needs', and it is thought that these should be satisfied for all equally before further desires are satisfied for any. 'Bread for all before there is jam for some.' The jam, however, is not distributed equally. On the other hand, the Liberal position is rarely carried to the extreme conclusion, 'each for himself and devil take the hindmost'. Few adherents of the position would be content to let the weak and the aged starve to death. Some sort of basic minimum, ranging from the paltry assistance of the Poor Law to the ambitions of the 'Beveridge Programme', is usually admitted, and this is a concession to the principle of equal satisfactions. Justice, then, is thought to require a basic minimum of equal satisfactions, unrelated to utility or to capacity. Above that line, room is left for individuals to do as they think fit. The position of the line is different in different societies and at different periods of history, depending both on economic circumstances and on the level of social morality. That it depends on economic circumstances is obvious enough. 'A chicken in every pot' is impossible if a country cannot afford to raise or buy enough chickens. But it depends on the level of social morality too. Tom Paine proposed in 1797 the establishment of a national fund, from which everyone should receive £15 at the age of 21 and £10 at the age of 50 'to enable them to live without wretchedness and go decently out of the world'.[7] The country could have afforded this very limited scheme of 'social security', depending as it did, like the Beveridge plan, on some redistribution of existing income, but most of the people who could influence social legislation at the time would have thought it wildly utopian. On the other hand, some people today would say that a Government which sticks to all the benefits of the Welfare State, irrespective of whether the country can afford them, is allowing its moral fervour to outrun economic necessity.

Distributive justice, we have found, makes two claims of equality, first, equality of opportunity, that is, the greatest possible degree of opportunity for all impartially; and second, the provision of material means to satisfaction for all impartially, such provision in practice being limited, for utilitarian reasons, to a standard of basic needs.

The first of these principles depends partly on utility (since the development and exercise of a good many capacities is useful for the production of means to satisfaction for society at large), and partly on valuing self-development. This means that the development of capacity is regarded as a moral claim, reinforced by the claims of utility if the capacity is especially useful to society (as, e.g., technical skill or teaching ability is and the capacity for playing chess is not), and overridden by the claim of utility if the capacity is socially harmful (e.g. the capacity for burglary; we do not think we ought to provide schools of burglary for potentially successful burglars). Since people differ in capacities, and since some men are better endowed than others with a particular capacity, this claim for the development of capacity is not one for equality (except in the sense that it is a claim of everyone) but reflects the differences of nature. We speak of '*equal* opportunity' because in the past the opportunities provided for development have not been in accordance with the inequalities of nature but have either run counter to them for the private interests of some or else exaggerated them for the sake of general interest. Where opportunity was not confined to privilege, it depended on social utility; it was extended to those whose development would benefit society to an unusual degree. Thus there is no need to invoke justice in order to approve of the provision of free higher education for the gifted children of poor parents; social utility will require it no less. But the provision of equal opportunity for the handicapped, in mind or body, can often not be justified by utility.

The second element of distributive justice ensures that there is a basic minimum for all even if some of those affected could not achieve it by their own efforts. Here we 'go against nature' in the sense that we rate basic needs above the capacity to satisfy them, and of course above social utility, for keeping alive the aged and the incurably sick is not economic. We think it is due to *them* as individuals.

The two principles of equality, like the principle of retributive justice, are chiefly concerned to protect the individual irrespective of general utility. One is a claim that each person be given such opportunity for development as his natural capacity allows, even though it may not always add to social utility (but we shall do still more for socially useful capacities because of their utility). The other is a claim for the satisfaction of basic needs (i.e. those regarded as essential for tolerable living) for each individual even though there may be no economic return. We think these two things are due to individuals as such, as being 'ends-in-themselves'. If, with Mill, we hold that the most important element in the idea of liberty is not the negative factor of the absence of restraint but the positive factor of valuing individuality, then the essential point of justice and that of liberty are identical.

4 Tensions between Equality and Freedom

i

Almost any aims or goals can conflict with each other at times, but the aims of equality and freedom seem especially liable to do so. Why? Basically because of natural inequality. Men are unequal in their natural powers; freedom to use unequal powers results in unequal achievement, which in turn increases the inequality of power. The goal of equality requires some restriction of the freedom of those who have superior power. In such circumstances equality conflicts with freedom because freedom nourishes natural inequality.

Needless to say, natural inequality is not the one and only source of tension between the goals of equality and freedom. Artificial inequality has the same effect as natural inequality and also gives rise to tension with freedom. For example, if Topsy inherits a million dollars, she has more power than Mopsy who inherits nothing. Unrestrained freedom to exert her monetary power will soon put Topsy still further ahead of Mopsy. A government that wants to narrow the gap between rich and poor, and in this sense to pursue the goal of equality, must limit the freedom of the rich. An inheritance tax that takes away from Topsy a good slice of her million dollars is a restriction on freedom. It restricts the freedom of Topsy's father to give Topsy all the benefits of his million dollars; and it restricts the amount of freedom that Topsy herself has to obtain the desirable things that money can buy. Of the inequalities among mankind, far more are artificial than natural; and therefore many people will want to argue that artificial inequality is far more important than natural inequality as a source of tension between the goals of equality and freedom, that in fact the role of natural inequality is relatively trivial. To this bone of contention I shall return later. For the moment let us simply note that natural inequality is certainly not a necessary condition of the tension with which we are concerned.

E

Nor is natural inequality a sufficient condition of such tension. We should not suppose that tension between the two goals is inevitable whenever there is inequality, either natural or artificial. If superiority of power, whether natural or artificial, is not used to the disadvantage of others, there is no reason to restrain it. In Charles Dickens's novel, *The Pickwick Papers*, Mr. Pickwick's servant Sam Weller is naturally superior to his employer in brain power, while Mr. Pickwick is artificially superior in monetary power. But since each of them is ready to use his superior power for the benefit of the other as well as of himself, the inequalities do no harm and call for no restraints on freedom, at any rate if we think simply of the mutual relations between these two men.

Freedom and equality can each of them take many forms, can each be exemplified in many different ways. One aspect of freedom can conflict with another aspect of freedom while being compatible with an aspect of equality. For instance, if John Doe has freedom to sing as loudly as he likes at all times of the day and night, he takes away the freedom of his neighbour Richard Roe to rest at peace. One man's treat is another man's prison. Yet John Doe's freedom is quite compatible with the equal freedom of Richard Roe to retaliate in kind. Equal freedom is an important aspect of equality and an important aspect of freedom. It serves both goals and involves no conflict between them. Equal freedom conflicts with absolute freedom, for it requires some restraint, i.e. some limitation of freedom; but despite this negative function of limiting freedom, equal freedom is still also a positive pursuit of the goal of freedom and is not a pursuit of the goal of equality alone. For when we talk of making equal freedom an aim, we mean a maximum of equal freedom, as much freedom as possible so long as there is the same amount of freedom for others. The goal of equal freedom is not just a limitation of existing unequal freedoms so as to bring everyone down to the same level; if it were, it would be indistinguishable from equal slavery. Equal freedom as a goal means seeking to *maximize* freedom for everyone equally. Nevertheless the pursuit of equal freedom does not get rid of tensions between equality and freedom. Equal freedom in one respect can conflict with freedom in another respect and it can also conflict with other kinds of equality. In the example that I gave just now, John Doe and Richard Roe had equal freedom to sing loudly at all times, but John's exercise of the freedom to sing conflicted with Richard's freedom to rest in peace and quiet. Again, if John likes singing and Richard loathes it, then their equal freedom to sing tends to go against their attainment of equal satisfactions.

A major focus of tension is between equality of opportunity and equality of satisfaction, and this can be represented as a tension between freedom and equality since equal opportunity is a form of equal freedom. Opportunity to develop and exercise one's potentialities is more than freedom from restraint by human beings; indeed it often requires active assistance by other human beings, in education or training, for example. But opportunity can still be called a form of freedom in a wider sense of that term, for opportunity is freedom *from* impediments that would otherwise stand in the way of self-fulfilment, and it is certainly freedom *to* achieve what one would like. Everybody, whatever his political persuasion, is in favour of equal opportunity, that is to say, a maximum of opportunity for all members of a society equally. This is a pursuit of the two goals of equality and freedom. But undoubtedly equal opportunity can conflict with other kinds of equality, and in fact this particular conflict is, in terms of present-day political attitudes, the most important example of tension between equality and freedom. It highlights the point made in my first paragraph. Equal opportunity (or freedom) to develop talents that are naturally unequal produces as a result unequal achievements.

The traditional ideology of the United States stands for equal opportunity: it says that anyone, if he has the natural ability, should have the opportunity to rise from log cabin to White House. No doubt it is not true in fact; national aspirations are never adequately translated into reality. But at any rate it is the aspiration, the American dream, and as a foreign observer I am led to think that the aspiration is not entirely mythical; in my opinion, there is in many respects more equality of opportunity in the United States than in most of the older countries of Western Europe. It does not follow, however, that American society is more equalitarian in general than, say, British society. If you think of the effect of taxation policy in reducing inequality of income and wealth; or if you think of the effect of a National Health Service in making an adequate level of medical care available to everyone irrespective of means; in these respects you will find that Britain is more equalitarian than the United States.

Consider the theory and practice of education. Equal opportunity for university education means that everybody capable of benefiting from a university education should have it. There should be no discrimination on grounds other than ability. No one should find entry difficult because of poverty, race, sex, religion, or anything else except the capacity to undertake a university course successfully. But discrimination on grounds of capacity there must be, if equal opportunity is to be preserved. I assume that the number of places available is bound to have a limit; otherwise there would be a waste of resources and so an unwarranted neglect of other goals that also need economic resources. Therefore there has to be some sort of selection of entrants to university. Selection by reference to capacity gives equal opportunity; it gives the opportunity to develop academic talent to everyone who has academic talent. It does not give that opportunity to the man who has no such talent; but nothing can give that man the opportunity to develop what he does not have.

This equal opportunity, however, has the result that unequal talent becomes unequal achievement. Tom has a talent for mathematics and Tim has not. Even without higher education Tom will be smarter than Tim in many jobs, but a university degree will add enormously to this difference. Difference does not necessarily mean inequality, and if Tim has a talent for popular entertainment he may get just as much satisfaction and material reward from that as Tom gets from the profession of accountancy or whatever. There would be little need to bother about natural inequalities if nature gave everyone a flair that met a demand. But that is not what happens. Some talents are relatively scarce and are in great demand. The people who have those talents will get rewards and powers beyond the average. Opportunity to develop the talent will increase the inequality.

The American devotion to equal opportunity has led to strenuous efforts to remove discrimination on irrelevant grounds such as race or sex. So much so indeed that there is some danger of running into the absurd consequence of discriminating against ability. A case that came before the U.S. Supreme Court in April 1974 concerned an action brought by Mr. Marco DeFunis against the

University of Washington, Seattle. Mr. DeFunis had applied to enter the Law School and had not been accepted, although he had a better record of academic and aptitude ratings than thirty-six other applicants who were admitted. These thirty-six were admitted because they were members of minority ethnic groups and because the Law School was making special efforts to include a decent proportion of minority groups in the intake. The Supreme Court decided by five to four that there was a technical reason against their giving a ruling. One member of the minority was Mr. Justice William Douglas, and in his dissenting opinion he said that Mr. DeFunis should be subject neither to any advantage nor to any disadvantage because he was white. 'Whatever his race, he has a constitutional right to have his application considered on its individual merits in a racially neutral manner.' Mr. Justice Douglas went on to say that a university was perfectly entitled to take account of barriers that faced minority applicants; it might judge, for example, that a black man, who started life in a ghetto and yet managed to reach minimum grades for admission to university, had shown evidence of high motivation and so of more than minimum capacity to benefit from university education. Still, the fact remains that the drive to remove unjustified discrimination on irrelevant grounds *can* lead to 'discrimination in reverse' against those who ought to be selected if relevant criteria are applied. The drive to remove one form of unequal opportunity can lead to introducing another form of it. Equal opportunity means ignoring artificial inequalities but following natural inequalities.[1]

ii

I now return to the question whether it is natural or artificial inequality that is the primary source of tension between the goals of equality and freedom. Inequality is of course not the same as difference. There can be natural differences between people without natural inequalities. The difference between male and female is a biological, a natural, difference, but it does not of itself imply any inequality, any superiority and inferiority. The same is true of the difference between pink skin, yellow skin, and brown skin. Similarly there can be artificial differences between people without artificial inequalities. The difference between a lawyer and a doctor is an artificial difference, and it does not of itself imply any inequality, any superiority and inferiority. Inequality is one kind of difference, a difference of degree in things of the same kind. A tall man and a small man are unequal in size; a rich man and a poor man are unequal in wealth. The first is a natural inequality, the second an artificial one.

Some natural differences of kind tend to go along with natural differences of degree in respect of some other quality. On average, men tend to be physically stronger than women. But this is only a tendency. The mere fact that John is a man and Joan is a woman does not guarantee that John can lift heavier weights than Joan, or therefore that John can be more useful than Joan as a farmworker, in consequence of which he should inevitably get a higher wage than Joan. There is a controversy whether the members of one ethnic group tend to be more intelligent than members of another ethnic group. But even if this thesis were clearly established, like the average difference of physical strength between men and women, the mere fact that Tom belongs to one ethnic group would be no guarantee whatsoever that he was more or less intelligent than Tim who belongs to a different ethnic group. Tendencies for groups do not determine the facts about particular individuals. They do, however, express facts about large numbers. Since physical strength is useful for most of the jobs on a farm, we can expect to find that male farmworkers will usually be offered higher pay than females. If the lower rate is *always* given to a woman, even to Joan who happens to be as strong as the average man, the discrimination is unjustified. If it is given only to those women who are less strong than the average man, it is justifiable on a relevant economic ground.

The tendency for women to be less physically strong than men is a natural inequality, as natural as other biological differences between the sexes that are differences of kind and so not inequalities. But the natural differences between the sexes—not only the greater physical strength of men but also the consequences of women's ability to produce children—have resulted in social differences that include inequalities more striking than the inequalities of nature. I do not say more striking than the *differences* of nature. None of the social (i.e. artificial) differences between men and women is more striking than their different functions in the process of procreation. But the artificial inequality between men and women that exists in practically all societies is far more striking than the natural tendency of men to be physically stronger, or psychologically more aggressive, than women. Even in the most equalitarian of societies, women are vastly outnumbered by men in positions of high authority or wealth. Despite all the efforts of social reform and progressive legislation, opportunity and other forms of freedom are less for women than for men.

Much the same can be said of social differences between ethnic groups in most (but not all) societies. In this case there is not even any hard evidence of a genuine natural inequality that gives rise to the artificial inequalities. Even if it should be scientifically established that differences of Intelligence Quotient among different ethnic groups in one society are determined more by heredity than by environment, we should still look to history rather than genetics to explain the social inequalities among the castes of India, or those among Americans with pink, reddish-brown, or brownish-black skins.

Social inequalities, then, are greater than, and are not much dependent on, the natural inequalities of human beings. Both of them produce tension between equality and freedom. If social or artificial inequality is greater than natural, will it not occasion the greater tension? Certainly it will occasion the greater movement for reform. But not necessarily the greater tension between equality and freedom. If an inequality is artificial, it can be removed by social action. If it is natural, it cannot. The success of a campaign to give women equal opportunities with men may mean a restriction of freedom for some men while enlarging freedom for women. Nobody likes to have his freedom restricted, so of course there is conservative opposition to such a campaign, as there is to any radical movement. But there is not, I suggest, a deep-rooted or lasting tension between goals. The essential justice of the campaign is manifest, and the opposition of male chauvinists will gradually wear down.

Is there any evidence of this? I think there is ample evidence in the history of equalitarian social reform. Right-wing political groups give the appearance of gradually moving to the left, they steal the clothes of their left-wing opponents. The Welfare State, once the programme of radicals, is now accepted by all political parties in the countries of Western Europe. A conservative politician in Britain could declare 'We are all socialists now', meaning that all parties now accepted measures that once were confined to socialists. This is not to say that conservatives are now just as radical as socialists in every way. But it is to say that some equalitarian programmes are now accepted by people who once opposed them. Privileged groups will grumble at the first proposal of laws to reduce inequality, whether by a redistribution of income and wealth, or by widening the scope of civil and political rights, or by restraining some forms of discrimination; but after a time nearly everyone accepts the laws as fair and proper. The people who used to be privileged no longer resent the reduction of their freedom, since they agree that the change was justified; the old inequalities were not warranted by any tolerable concept of justice. This is because the inequalities in question were not based on relevant differences of capacity or merit.

Such a concession of freedom for the sake of equality is less likely, however, where natural inequalities are concerned. An extreme equalitarian may say that nature's unequal distribution of brains or beauty is unfair and that social arrangements should try to compensate, perhaps by requiring all children to have the same kind of education, or by forbidding the marriage of a younger sister before an older. But the clever and the beautiful will not reconcile themselves easily to a stultifying of their natural gifts. Artificial inequality can be artificially removed; natural inequality cannot. Some natural inequalities can be mitigated or compensated by artificial means: spectacles can mitigate, but not cure, short sight; a tribal dowry can bring to an ugly girl a husband, but not a train of admirers. Any attempt to remove natural inequalities is vain and is therefore resented by those whose freedom it curtails. It cannot lead to a levelling up, since natural defects cannot, for the most part, be made good; so it results simply in a levelling down, in depriving the naturally fortunate of the benefits of their natural gifts.

I must repeat that the extent of artificial inequality is far greater than that of natural inequality. All that I have said about the difference between them does not mean that it is *easy* to get rid of artificial inequality. The long, persistent efforts of social reformers, the eruptions of social revolution, when directed to the goal of equality, have almost always been attacking artificial inequalities. My argument is simply that the tension between equality and freedom does not endure when the drive for equality aims at the removal of artificial inequalities; it does endure when the drive for equality is directed at natural inequalities. That is why I maintain that natural inequality is the basic cause of the tension that seems especially liable to persist between the two goals of equality and freedom.

iii

In the history of political thought we often find statements that all men are by nature both free and equal. Usually these are normative statements, meaning that men ought to be free and equal, with the implication that in fact they are not. There is, however, at least one important exception. When Hobbes says that in a state of nature all men would be free and equal, he is not speaking normatively. He is not describing an actual situation either, for his state of nature is largely hypothetical. Nevertheless his statement is positive, not normative. When Hobbes speaks of natural freedom (or natural right) he means the absence of norms, both legal and moral. When he speaks of natural equality he means a rough equality of abilities. He allows that there are differences of degree in the capacities of different men, but he says that these cancel each other out; if one man is physically stronger than another, the second may be superior in cunning; for all that it matters, there is a rough equality. Nobody can suppose that Hobbes was subject to idealistic illusion. Is not he therefore a powerful witness for the view that natural inequalities are relatively trivial and do not count?

No, Hobbes is not a witness for that view in our present discussion. For our discussion is concerned with social relations, while Hobbes is concerned with political. When Hobbes says that all men are by nature roughly equal in abilities, his point is that no one person is capable of dominating simply by natural powers. No human being, he reminds us, has the irresistible power that is attributed to God. The power of God is so far superior to that of all else as to be irresistible, and therefore the natural kingdom of God, Hobbes says, rests on natural power. The differences of ability among men are puny in comparison; no single person has the natural power to dominate, and so political control must rest on artifice. Leviathan, the State, is an artificial (and mortal) god, that has to be kept in being by will, by deliberate measures. The focus of interest in Hobbes's theory is very firmly the political rather than the social structure. In the domain of political ideas there is tension between freedom and authority, and perhaps between equality and efficiency. But the tension between freedom and equality does not impinge directly on the main problems of politics; it shows itself in the wider area of social ideas.

Hobbes is right to play down the importance of natural inequality for the problems of politics. His positive view of equality differs radically from the normative view incorporated into the theory of democracy, but the practice of democracy bears out the truth of Hobbes's opinion. Democratic institutions assume a rough natural equality when it comes to working the political machine. Nobody supposes that the ability to exercise judgement on political issues is equal in all adults; but still, numbers count for more than do individual differences. The combined wisdom of the many is more reliable, for political purposes, than the wisdom of the few, even though the few be more enlightened individually than the many. This is recognized by Aristotle, who is as shrewd in his appreciation of democracy's strength as he is of its weaknesses. Political decisions have to take account of the wishes of the majority, for in the last resort the power of the State depends on their (at least passive) consent. Democracy in theory has a normative appeal; democracy in practice rests on hard facts. The growth of democracy is like the decline of slavery. Men of good will condemn slavery for its denial of the norm of freedom; but slavery declined in advancing societies because it was economically less efficient than wage labour subject to market forces. Adam Smith brought this out very clearly at an early stage of his economic thinking.

Equality and freedom are both norms of democracy. So far as freedom is concerned, democracy has no monopoly. Most political doctrines claim to believe in freedom, though some of the anti-democratic views have to give freedom a peculiar interpretation in order to back up their claim. The belief in equality, too, is not necessarily confined to democrats, as the example of Hobbes shows, but equality is not so universal a goal as is freedom. The distinctive feature of democratic theory is to join equality and freedom and to put them both at the forefront of its political ideal. In that context there is no suggestion of a clash between them. For the democrat, they go together. Critics of democracy also do not find any objection to the linkage as such. They attack equality as unrealistic; they attack the democratic concept of freedom as dangerous; but they are not worried by any incompatibility between the two. The incompatibility appears rather in debate about relative priorities *within* a democratic system. Conservatives and Liberals express the fear that socialist emphasis on equality will stifle freedom; they are the people who emphasize the tension between the concepts and the need to check the pursuit of equality for that reason. Socialists, while sharing a belief in democracy, tend to dismiss these fears or else to say that the tension affects only those kinds of freedom (such as economic laissez-faire) that are not particularly valuable anyway. Each of the two sides resolves the tension by giving priority to its favoured goal.

The dispute makes a difference to the economic and social policies followed by the parties, and those policies will indeed affect the character of a democratic régime. They do not, however, determine whether or not it is a democratic régime. The difference between free-enterprise capitalism and equalitarian socialism is a difference of socio-economic rather than of political structure. Of course it enters deeply into the disputes between political parties and is political in that sense. Nevertheless a man is not a democrat or an anti-democrat because he favours liberty over equality or equality over liberty. To be a democrat he must take both as worthy goals. To be an anti-democrat he must reject at least one. The anti-democrat therefore has no problem of tension between the two. Tension between two goals can arise only for someone who accepts both as goals. The tension between equality and liberty is a problem *within* democracy.

Both liberty and equality are social values in the sense that they have to do with individuals in relation to others. There would be no point in talking of freedom or equality for a man who chose to live alone on a desert island. When we speak of a man's freedom or unfreedom we mean the absence or presence of restraint upon him by other persons; when we speak of his equality or inequality we are comparing or contrasting him with his fellows. Yet there is a sense in which we can describe freedom as an individual value and equality as a social value. Although freedom has to do with a man's relation to other people, what is *valued* in freedom is the scope that it gives to the individual person—to do what he likes, to exercise choice, to develop his talents, or even to go to rack and ruin. In the case of equality, the comparison with others enters into the thing valued; the similarity between different individuals is what is valued and sought. This difference between the two concepts can contribute to tension between them. People who see the individual person as the ultimate locus of ethical value are more or less bound to give priority to freedom over equality in the event of conflict. Those who do not may be ready to prefer equality.

How, you may ask, can democrats come into the second category? We are talking of debate within the circle of democratic ideas. Do not all democrats see the individual person as the ultimate locus of ethical value? Not necessarily. Modern democratic thought has a trinity of values: liberty, equality, fraternity. The third of these fastens on the inter-personal relation of brotherly love, and there is an impressive line of thought in moral philosophy which says that the value of human existence always lies in inter-personal relations. It is possible to bring the value of freedom under such a conception, though only at the expense of some straining and even, I would say, distortion. At any rate one can be a democrat without believing that *all* ethical value attaches in the last resort to individuality. On a straightforward view, liberty is an individual value while equality and fraternity are social values. Non-democratic societies that lack a strong tradition of freedom for the individual, assume without question that, in case of conflict, liberty should give way to family or social solidarity; and when such societies have undergone an equalitarian revolution and have adopted democratic values, they still tend to think of liberty as less important than equality and fraternity.

In a conflict between the individual value of liberty and the social values of equality and fraternity, it seems to me that equality has a less secure standing than fraternity. When we think about the foundation of our values, we can make a case for freedom in terms of the essential character of human personality. Every person has desires and potentialities. He cannot exist as a person unless he satisfies many of his desires. He cannot be his 'real self' unless he can develop his potentialities. These things are basic to human personality, and freedom is valued as their necessary condition. A case for fraternity, too, can be made in terms of the essence of human personality, though not everyone will accept this line of thought. We can say that love and service to others are essential to human existence in that a life without them is so much less rich, feels so much less fulfilled. But what about equality? It does not seem at all sensible to say that equality is essential for a properly human existence. The gross inequality of master and slave is an inhuman situation, but this is because the slave lacks freedom, not because of inequality as such. Critics of equalitarianism often say that it rests on envy, a fact of life but not one to which we should want to attach high value. The criticism is somewhat unfair, for the goal of equality, like other aspects of justice, is a universalization of individual feeling and has thereby been detached from reference to oneself alone. Equality is sought in the name of justice, as something required by rationality, an insistence on like treatment for like cases. Still, even that does not seem to go to the core of human personality in the way that freedom does. On this score, therefore, freedom appears to be a greater value than equality. Tension between liberty and fraternity is more difficult to resolve, and because fraternity goes along with equality, the tension between fraternity and liberty appears to add to the tension between equality and liberty.

iv

Democracy in ancient Greece did not have the modern trinity of democratic values. Although social solidarity was a prominent feature of the moral outlook of all ancient Greeks, the specific concept of social fraternity arises from the Judaeo-Christian theology of a universal father. Athenian democracy linked liberty and equality with a different third value, variety. In a discussion of equality on the Radio 3 network of the B.B.C., Sir Isaiah Berlin surprisingly said that variety was a modern value and was not to be found among advocates of equality in the ancient world. It is true that we have no work of Greek political philosophy advocating variety along with liberty and equality. But this is simply because we have no work of Greek political philosophy advocating democracy. We do have works attacking democracy, and from their attacks we can learn what democrats valued. Plato's *Republic* speaks of liberty, equality, and variety as the main features of a democracy, features in which the democrat took pride. While fraternity is linked to equality, variety is linked to liberty. Freedom displays variety. Freedom for individuals to do their own thing, to express their own wishes, to develop their own personalities, brings out the differences among them. Variety is not necessarily opposed to equality but it is certainly opposed to uniformity. It is easy to confuse equality with uniformity. Some equalitarians, and many critics of equalitarianism, are guilty of this confusion. They suppose that equality is the same as uniformity, and so they suppose that equality is in conflict with variety. And since variety is undoubtedly connected with freedom, they are led to think that a conflict of uniformity with variety is a conflict of equality with freedom. Here is a source of apparent tension between the goals of equality and freedom, but one that rests on misunderstanding.

I have already pointed out that inequality is not the same as difference. Two people can be different in kind without being unequal. Inequality is a difference of degree in respect of a sameness of kind. Equality is the contradictory of this, the absence of a difference of degree in respect of a sameness of kind. Since all men share some samenesses of kind, some common qualities, equality among them involves some sameness of degree also. The social goal of equality, however, does not require that all men should have the same degree of *all* qualities that they have in common, still less that they should be made to share all possible common qualities, which is what uniformity would mean. Equalitarians do not seek, or even yearn, to make all men exactly the same height. If we take social equality as a goal, we are not worried about the differences between people in respect of height or in lots of other ways. Our concern is with certain things that are valued or disvalued and are susceptible of regulation. We shall want to provide similar opportunities for people of similar ability, similar satisfactions for people with similar needs. We shall not want to act as if everyone had the same kind and degree of ability or need. That is to say, we shall not assume uniformity of abilities or needs, let alone uniformity in other respects.

However, we do assume some relevant similarities among all human beings, and this is why it is possible, both for advocates and for critics of equalitarianism, to confuse the goal of equality with that of uniformity. We assume that all human beings are similar in having certain basic needs which ought to be satisfied for all equally. We assume that all human beings have capacities which other animals do not have, and that these capacities should be given opportunity for development and use. But to say that everyone needs medical care is not to say that everyone needs to have his appendix removed; and to say that everyone should be educated is not to say that everyone should study ancient Greek. Unfortunately such truisms can be overlooked. The man who is anxious to remove privilege in education may come to think this implies that everyone should go to the same sort of school; while his critics may think he is saying (sometimes he really is!) that everyone should have the same sort of education.

There is a logical connection between equality and uniformity in that uniformity means sameness in every respect while equality means sameness in some limited respect. It does not follow, however, that every single species of equality is a step on the road to uniformity. Few people would confuse equal opportunity with uniformity, since equal opportunity tends to enhance natural differences and to stimulate variety. There is no tension between equal opportunity and variety, any more than between equal opportunity and freedom. Equality has to go against natural differences before it can even seem to wear the mantle of uniformity. The equalitarian does sometimes want to go against nature, for instance when he tries to compensate for natural disabilities. And because these disabilities are departures from the norm of human nature, he may be led to say that his aim is to restore what is truly natural. The concept of nature and the natural is used both positively and normatively, both for all that comes about without human intervention and for selected examples that happen to be perfect of their kind. A concentration upon the latter can indeed lead to the desire to make all examples conform to the perfect instance. I do not think, however, that this kind of attitude has much to do with equalitarianism. Plato and Aristotle both took a normative view of nature and applied it to human life and social institutions as to everything else; but in their case this approach to ethics and politics went along with opposition to equalitarianism. The Stoics inherited from them the normative concept of life according to nature and also believed in human equality; yet one cannot say that the Stoics thereby remedied any *inconsistency* in the ethics of Plato and Aristotle.

The motives that lead men to equalitarianism do not seem to me to include a liking for uniformity. People who like uniformity do so either for aesthetic or for economic reasons. They may think that diversity is messy and distracting, while simplicity or the repetition of a regular pattern pleases the sense of order. Alternatively they may think that uniformity makes for fewer problems; diversity is less amenable to control. Plato's disapproval of variety seems to have been aesthetic; Stalin's was economic. Perhaps the two attitudes are connected; perhaps the reason why simplicity and regular pattern are aesthetically pleasing is that they make it easier for us to grasp and remember a multitude of data, they make it easier for us to cope. But there is still an important difference, in that aesthetic 'coping' is a matter of contemplation, while what I have called the economic preference for uniformity arises from the desire for practical control. The second is more liable to lead to tyranny. However, neither of these motives for seeking uniformity has had much to do with equalitarianism. The equalitarian is almost always driven by a sense of justice and a feeling that there are injustices to be righted. Now the sense of justice may be held to originate from more than one source in human psychology—resentment, envy, compassion; but all are quite different from the sources of an aesthetic or an economic preference for uniformity. Only too often the sense of justice is in conflict both with aesthetic and with economic values.

Freedom and variety differ from equality in this respect. Freedom and variety both have an aesthetic attraction. Freedom, and the individuality that goes with it, are essential for artistic creation and appear to have a creative element in their own essence. Variety, we say, is the spice of life, and unity in variety appeals to the sense of beauty rather more than simple regularity of pattern. As for economic values, while efficiency often requires planning and control, we all recognize the force of Adam Smith's contention that in economic life proper 'the obvious and simple system of natural liberty' contributes most to the growth of real wealth.

I do not think, however, that the contrast between freedom and equality in this regard has anything to do with tension between them. So far as our subject is concerned, the relevance of this discussion about variety and uniformity is as follows. There is obviously a tension between variety and uniformity. Freedom is closely connected with variety. Equality has a logical link with uniformity and is therefore liable to be confused with it, although being in fact substantially different. Consequently the genuine tension between variety and uniformity is liable to be interpreted as a form of tension between freedom and equality. I have argued that this is an error, due to the confusion between equality and uniformity.

In the course of this essay I have tried to deal with four possible sources of tension: (1) natural inequality; (2) artificial inequality; (3) the difference between freedom as an individual value and equality as an inter-personal value; and (4) the relation of freedom and equality to variety and uniformity. I have suggested that the first of these four is a more basic and a more lasting source of tension than the second, although the second is far more important as a spur to equalitarian reform. The third is a contributory factor but not, I think, one of great significance. The fourth leads to confusing a real tension elsewhere with an apparent one between freedom and equality.

F

5 Conservative and Prosthetic Justice

The adjectives in my title are deliberately intended to recall dental as well as political connotations. Traditionalists may think of prosthetic justice as a mere artificial substitute for the genuine natural product, while radicals may think of conservative justice as hidebound.

LAW AND MORALS

The term 'justice' is used both of law and of morals. In the law, justice covers the whole field of the principles laid down, the decisions reached in accordance with them, and the procedures whereby the principles are applied to individual cases. The system of law *is* justice in the legal sense of the term. In morals, justice covers only part of the field of judgement and action; justice is contrasted with generosity or charity, this being moral action that goes beyond mere justice. Since the law does not try to, and indeed logically could not, enforce the higher morality of generosity, but confines itself within the domain of moral justice (which is not to say that it necessarily reaches the limits of that domain), it is intelligible that the law should use the term 'justice' to describe the whole of its own operations.

Two processes, of conservation and reformation, can be seen clearly enough in the field of law. The first task of a system of law is to preserve an existing order of rights and duties. Like other preservatives, an established system of law tends to produce rigidity. The rights and duties that it protects and requires are those of a past morality. Changes in moral notions, or in the conditions to which moral notions are applied, lead to a demand that the law be changed in the name of (new notions of) justice or fairness. Thus the Common Law of England, which began as official declaration and enforcement of common practice and common belief about rights and duties, became in time a backward-looking system of precedents, and had to be modified by the application of rules of Equity, that is to say, principles of current thought about justice. In due course, the courts administering Equity became themselves equally stiff with precedent, so that now Common Law includes their findings as well, and the whole system of case law has to be modified by Statute. Broadly speaking, Common Law conserves the moral ideas of the past, while Statute reforms and adds to Common Law in the light of the moral ideas of the present.

If what I have said of law is true, it will follow that moral notions themselves are subject to a similar process of modification, and no one will be surprised at the suggestion that, within the sphere of morals also, the concept of justice is used to cover both the conservation of traditional ideas and the modification of these by new ideas. What I want to argue is that this process of development includes a gradual clarification of the concept of justice, and enables us to sift the elements of justice proper from elements of utility.

But before I can proceed to my main problem, I must justify the assumption I have made that one can compare a discussion of the moral notion of justice with a discussion of law. Some people will deny this, saying that law is 'objective' while justice is 'subjective'; you and I are not free to decide what is the law, but we are free to decide what we shall count as just; judges decide the law, but in the sphere of morality every man may be his own judge.

In fact it is not true that only judges decide the law. When judges decide what the law is, they are often determining what it shall be; and this function is of course not exclusively theirs. Legislatures decide what a part of the law shall be, and in so far as you and I can influence the legislature, we can help, in a small way, to determine what the law shall be. Still, the point remains that once legislatures and judges have decided, their decisions are authoritative. In the sphere of morals, it is said, no one can assert that your views or mine shall not be followed. Can we then speak of any firm concept of justice?

EVERY MAN HIS OWN JUDGE?

'In those days', concludes the Book of Judges sorrowfully, 'there was no king in Israel: every man did that which was right in his own eyes.' It may seem strange that the last sentence should count as a reproach. That a man should follow the judgement of his own conscience seems essential to morality, though we may well be troubled when his conscience is so perverted as to deny to other people rights which are almost universally acknowledged. My own view[1] is that in *such* circumstances a man's duty is *not* what his conscience says; for A's duty to B corresponds to B's right against A, and I should not allow that the rights of B always depend on the thought of those against whom he claims a right. Some will disagree, if we are seeking only to determine what is A's *duty*, and will deny that A's duty corresponds to B's right. But if we shift the discussion to the determination of rights, that is to say, of justice,[2] the position implied by the biblical quotation may receive wider acceptance. It is not open to any individual to decide for himself what are the rights of others, i.e. whether his action towards them is just.

Some will still disagree. As an example, let me cite Hans Kelsen. I cite him *honoris causa*, for I regard his theory of law and the State as the most important contribution of the twentieth century to political theory. We may ask what is law, says Kelsen, but we may not ask what is justice, for justice is a subjective notion; different individuals and groups all have their own ideas of justice, and there is no way of deciding between them. This view of Kelsen's about justice depends partly on a similar account of all value-judgements, an account which is less likely to find credence today than in the 1920s and 1930s. It no doubt also depends partly on the fact that there *are* different ideas of justice. If we begin with Aristotle, for example, as so many theorists have done, we find that he distinguishes three or four different concepts. In the first place, Aristotle says, the term 'justice' may be applied to the whole of a universe of discourse about right and wrong, or to only part of such a universe. This is more or less the same as the contrast I have already noted between legal and moral justice. Then again, Aristotle distinguishes between distributive, remedial, and commutative (or 'reciprocal') justice. And then, as regards distributive justice itself, he distinguishes between a principle of distribution on the basis of merit (aristocratic justice) and a principle of distribution on the basis of equality (democratic justice). Other theorists seem to make a rather different distinction between two principles of distributive justice, distribution according to merit and distribution according to need. Then again, Marx, following some of the French socialists, narrows down or alters the concept of merit to that of work, and distinguishes the two principles of distribution as: 'to each according to his work' and 'to each according to his needs'. All these different ideas are said to be ideas of justice. How then can we speak of *one* concept? My contention will be that these different notions are not the unrelated ideas of different groups, but fit together so as to manifest the evolution of a single concept.

PLATO'S CONCEPT OF JUSTICE

I propose now to spend a little time on a side-issue, which, I think, corroborates my contention although at first sight it appears not to do so. In addition to the two causal factors which I have already mentioned, Kelsen's conclusion about justice owes something, I believe, to the influence of Plato. Plato's concept of justice seems quite remote from familiar uses of the term. Yet it is presented in the *Republic* as being so readily acceptable to Socrates' audience that one is apt to suppose it must be in line with at any rate one main strand of Greek thought. In a sense this is true, in another sense not. If Plato's concept of justice be treated as a version of 'aristocratic justice', it is indeed consonant with a strand not only of Greek thought but of the thought of other civilizations. If, however, we take his actual definition of justice literally, it is peculiar to Plato.

Yet does not he himself tell us that it is shared by others? The definition is given in Book IV (433b): justice is doing one's own job. In the text as we have it, Socrates is made to say: 'That justice is doing one's own job and not being a busybody, we have heard from many others and have often said ourselves.' Then, after receiving ready agreement to this statement, Socrates continues: 'Well, it somehow happens to have turned out that doing one's own job is justice'—a rather odd way, when you come to think about it, of putting an apparently unnecessary repetition.

Commentators have asked, *where* has it previously been said, by Plato or by others, in the literature which has come down to us, that justice is doing one's own job and not being a busybody. James

Adam, in the commentary of his edition of the *Republic*, gives us the answer: nowhere. It is not said earlier in the *Republic*, nor in any previous dialogue of Plato. (This definition of justice is given in one other dialogue attributed to Plato, *Alcibiades I*, at 127c. But *Alcibiades I* is almost certainly not a genuine work of Plato himself. It is evidently a late work, written by a disciple of Plato, and its definition of justice is simply following the doctrine of the *Republic*.) Nor does anyone else, including Aristotle, report that this is a common definition of justice.

Most people who have raised the question have been a little puzzled but have left it at that, assuming that the idea must have been common, though we have no record of it. Adam, however, refuses to be so easily put off. He notes that in the *Charmides*, 161b ff., 'doing one's own job' is given as the definition of *sophrosyne* (which we tend to translate as 'self-control' or 'temperance' or, in a social context, 'discipline'). There is also a passage in the *Timaeus* which suggests the same thing. Adam, therefore, conjectures that the word 'justice' (*dikaiosyne*) in *Republic* 433a9 is a scribe's error for an original reading of *sophrosyne*. The error, if it is one, is explained easily enough. The scribe would not remember the passage in the *Charmides*; he would simply know that 'doing one's own job' is the emphatic definition of justice in the *Republic*, and so he would think that *sophrosyne* was a previous scribe's error for *dikaiosyne*. Adam then points out that if we restore *sophrosyne* as the true reading, the whole passage makes better sense. For now this is how the conversation goes:

'It seems to me that justice is what we spoke of earlier, or something like it. We frequently said, if you remember, that each man should do one job, the job to which he is naturally suited.'

'Yes, we did say that.'

'*And yet* (the Greek is Καὶ μὴν . . . γε) we have heard from many others and we ourselves have often said that doing one's own job and not being over-busy is *self-control* (or discipline).'

'True enough.'

'Well, my friend, it somehow happens to have turned out that this business of doing one's own job is *justice*.'

This makes better sense, but there is more to it than Adam's concern simply with the sense of the passage. In the *Charmides*, the definition of *sophrosyne*, as minding your own business and not

meddling in other people's affairs, is attributed to Critias. Charmides and Critias were both aristocratic relations of Plato on his
mother's side, who became members of the oligarchic government
called the Thirty Tyrants and who tried to persuade Plato to join
them. It is natural enough for a person of aristocratic or oligarchic
tendencies to define *sophrosyne* (self-control or temperance), when
turned into a social virtue, as minding your own business and not
being a busybody. Being a busybody (*polypragmosyne*), poking
your nose into other people's business, was a common charge
levelled against the Athenian democrat by his oligarchic critics.
The oligarch or aristocrat wants everyone to keep to his proper
station, thereby producing a well-ordered or disciplined State, akin
to the disciplined nature of a self-controlled or temperate man.
What Plato does is to take over this aristocratic sentiment, and
make it seem more palatable by labelling it 'justice' instead of
'discipline' or 'order'; for the virtue of justice had come to have the
highest rank in the scale of social values, a rank formerly occupied,
in the days of heroic society, by the virtue of courage. It is a com-
monplace that the *Republic* makes justice and temperance almost
indistinguishable. This is why Plato's concept of justice is peculiar
to himself. Yet in a sense he is following a traditional strand of
thought, the aristocratic concept of justice as depending on merit.
That men's status in society should depend on their qualities, the
best men being at the top and the worst at the bottom, is familiar
aristocratic doctrine.

I am not implying that the novelty of Plato's doctrine of justice
is wholly determined by a political motive. When he speaks of
'justice' in the individual, he wants to deepen the common conception of morality, so as to make it include the spirit in which an
action is done as well as the external character of the act itself. This
also means that the concept of justice is widened to extend over
the whole field of morality instead of being confined to one class of
moral actions. The practice of extending a concept beyond its
normal connotations is both common and proper in philosophy.
I have therefore no complaint to make of Plato on that score. All I
contend at the moment is that Plato's peculiar use of the term
'justice' should not be taken to be that of the ancient Greeks, any
more than Berkeley's peculiar use of the term 'existence' should be
taken to be that of eighteenth-century Irishmen.

CONSERVATIVE AND PROSTHETIC JUSTICE

If we want to know what were the common conceptions of justice among the Greeks, we should go to Aristotle rather than Plato for our evidence. And when we do look at Aristotle's account of different conceptions of justice, we find that they are not far removed from those of our own civilization. That is why so many theorists find it convenient to make Aristotle's distinctions their starting point for the analysis of justice.

Let us look first at Aristotle's distinction between distributive, remedial, and commutative justice. The last two can, I think, be called conservative. Their object is to preserve an existing order of rights and possessions, or to restore it when any breaches have been made. We may add, though Aristotle does not, that penal justice likewise aims at conserving the general social order, as remedial and commutative justice aim at conserving the position of individuals within that order.

It is worth noting that while penal and remedial justice describe the work of the law, commutative justice goes beyond what the law requires and enforces. The remedial justice of law will rectify breaches of contract, but says nothing about the fairness of contracts themselves. Now a contract is fair when there is an exchange of equal value on each side. The law does not enforce this principle of fairness in the making of contracts. It allows, within pretty wide limits, free play to the self-interested forces of the market, and tells the buyer that he must look out for himself, as the vendor does. Many an unfair contract is made, in which there is not an equal exchange of value, but the law will not declare it invalid on that account. In the conditions of a free market, there is no protection of the existing position of individuals, in terms of the value of their possessions, by enforcing the rule of justice, except in so far as there is some restriction of unfair practices, and that implies some restriction of a free market.

It may be said that although conservative justice has little place in the market, where fortunes can be made and lost quickly, the forces of the market nevertheless give effect to the principle of merit. Luck comes in, of course, but to a large extent the man who makes a fortune does so by his ability and consequently 'deserves' his fortune. This is true enough. In conditions of competition, ability tends to succeed. Whether this should be called just is another question. For the moment let us suppose that it should. Penal, remedial, and commutative justice, then, are all conservative. It seems reasonable to say that distributive justice aims at modifying the *status quo*, and so may be called prosthetic justice. The modification may be made on the basis of merit, or of need, or of equality.

MERIT

If the reward of merit is a form of prosthetic justice, must not we say the same of penalties for demerit? This would imply that punishment, like other penalties, is a form of prosthetic justice. Reward and punishment seem to be opposite sides of the same coin, and if so, what goes for the one must go for the other. Yet surely punishment is a device for conserving an existing order of rules conferring duties and rights. This is true whether we think of punishment as deterrence or as retribution. (I ignore the reformative theory of punishment as based on confusion.)

Professor Ralf Dahrendorf, in an inaugural lecture 'On the Origin of Inequality' (printed as Essay 5 in *Philosophy, Politics and Society, Second Series* (1962), edited by Peter Laslett and W. G. Runciman), sets out a thesis which is of relevance here. Every society, he says, must have a set of norms, backed by sanctions which reward those who conform to the norms and penalize those who deviate. The purpose of the sanctions is to preserve the set of norms or values by which that society stands. This thesis couples reward with punishment and would assign both to what I am calling conservative justice. Of course the rewarding of merit alters the existing rights or status of individuals; but it conserves the existing system of social values, as does the punishment of crime.

I think we can bring out this point more clearly by considering the extent to which the rewarding of merit can be justified by utility. When we say that something is useful, we may mean that it prevents a loss of existing value, in which case it is plainly conservative. Alternatively, we may mean that it leads to an addition to the stock of value. In one sense this is prosthetic; for, as I have said, it is *adding* to what exists. In another sense it is conservative, in that the *kind* of value which is added, is the same as that which already exists, and is esteemed as an established value of the society concerned.

When we say that it is just to reward merit, what sort of merit do we have in mind? There are three possibilities. We may mean moral merit, or natural talent, or the exercise of industry. Marx's 'socialist' principle of distribution according to 'work' confines merit to the last of the three. I shall now take these three kinds of merit in the reverse order.

First, we often say it is just to reward industry and to penalize laziness. This principle plainly can, and indeed must, be justified on grounds of utility. Suppose a man were busily industrious at a useless task, like counting the number of grains in every heap of sand he could lay his hands on. Or suppose his industry were always directed to socially harmful tasks, like breaking up all the gas and water supply pipes he could get at. Should we think he deserved any reward? Industry is approved and rewarded only when, and because, it is socially useful. The reward itself, and similarly the penalizing of idleness, are also instruments of utility in encouraging the industrious to continue and the idle to follow their example.

Secondly, what of the reward of talent? Why is it just to benefit those who are already blessed by nature, and not those whom nature has left in the lurch? 'To him that hath shall be given.' This is what happens, but is it fair? Here again, surely, it may be useful, but it is not just. And here again, it is the useful talents that most obviously call for 'reward'. If a man has a talent for surgery, we think he should be given opportunity to develop it, and then be paid well for exercising it. But we shall not think the same of a talent for cracking safes.

Utility is not, however, the only reason for giving a man opportunity to develop and exercise his natural talents. We should wish to deny the opportunity to the cracksman, because the exercise of his talent is positively harmful. But suppose a talent is more or less neutral in its effect on others, e.g. a talent for chess-playing or for mountaineering (if we exclude supposed effects on national prestige). We are likely to spend money on training schools for surgeons before spending it on training schools for chess-players, because the surgeons will be useful to us. But if we can afford both, we shall think that the socially useless (though not the socially harmful) talent should be given training, simply because the individual who has the talent will be happier, will feel that he has realized himself, when he can exercise his talent to the full. We should say, I think, that we owe it to him as an individual, and that he has a moral right to such self-development. This is to say that it is a claim of justice.

What then of the *ranking* of talents? Why do we say that the man with a talent for surgery is blessed by nature, while the man who can find self-development in fretwork is less blessed? We have seen that the former talent is rewarded over the latter because of its greater utility. Must not we say the same of the initial ranking of the talents themselves? The potential surgeon is called blessed by nature because he can benefit his fellows and because he will in consequence be well rewarded and highly regarded. But then what of the talent of an artist? His abilities are not so obviously *useful* as is the talent of a surgeon, nor can he usually expect high rewards. Well, I think that here too the rating does lie in utility of a kind. What we call great art is art that we think will give lasting pleasure to many over a long period of time, though it is true that the artist often cannot expect much material reward or even much recognition in his own lifetime. One is tempted to say that he himself will have great happiness or a greater sense of self-fulfilment than will the fret-worker, quite apart from the pleasure that his work can give to others. Are we justified in saying this? I do not know. At any rate, it seems to me that at least *part* of the differential rating accorded to talent depends on utility, and that the residual claim of justice, the claim of the individual to self-development, *may* not admit of being rated higher or lower than the like claim of another. It is at least possible, then, that the residual claim of justice is an equal one for all human beings.

Thirdly, moral merit. What justifies the rewarding of virtue? Do not we say that virtue is its own reward? We judge nevertheless that virtue ought to be rewarded, but we should hesitate to put this judgement in the form that the virtuous man has a right to be rewarded, for to think of the reward as a right tarnishes the merit of the virtue. All this suggests that the rewarding of virtue is not called for as a matter of justice. On the other hand it is certainly called for as a matter of utility. Morally virtuous actions are those intended to benefit others, while morally vicious actions are those intended to harm others; and since the intentions of action are, more often than not, given effect by the actions they direct, virtuous actions tend to be useful and vicious actions tend to be harmful. Reward of the one, and punishment of the other, are themselves useful in encouraging people to follow the example of the virtuous and avoid that of the vicious.

I have argued here that the rewarding of virtue is justified by utility. While I have referred also to the utility of punishment, I should enter the *caveat* that in the case of punishment I think utility alone is insufficient justification. Punishment and reward, despite initial appearances, are not on all fours. Although we say that virtue is in a sense its own reward, we do not say that vice is similarly its own punishment. And while most of us would hesitate to speak of a right of the vicious to be punished, this is not for a reason parallel to that which inhibits us from speaking of a right of the virtuous to be rewarded. Indeed, some people (including some wrongdoers) think it is eminently proper to speak of a right to be punished. Two further differences may be mentioned. Everyone, I imagine, whatever his opinion about a right to be punished, would be ready to say that punishment is designed to meet the right of victims to be protected. Justice comes in again in upholding the right of the innocent not to be subjected to the pains imposed as punishment on the guilty. Neither this right nor that of victims has a correlate when rewards are considered.

A further *caveat* is that, though I have spoken of the utility of virtue as well as of the utility of reward, I do not imply that utility constitutes the whole value of virtue itself. The value of moral action, like the value of the exercise of talent, lies not only in utility but also in the direct realization of human worth. In the case of virtue, however, this means the realization of fellowship, and not, as with the exercise of talent, self-realization, unless we follow the Idealists in making the 'real self' go beyond the individual agent.

So far as the rewarding of merit is concerned, my conclusion, about all three types of merit, is that the ground of differential reward is utility. I have said that utility alone is not enough to justify punishment, but I have also noted that the complications which arise in the theory of punishment do not imply that there are correlative non-utilitarian factors affecting the reward of virtue.

EQUALITY AND NEED[3]

I turn now to the alternative claimants to the title of distributive justice, equal distribution and distribution according to need. At first sight, these seem to be distinct. Distribution according to need, like distribution according to merit, is a differential distribution. The man with the greater need is given more benefits and fewer burdens than the man with less need.

In fact, however, differential distribution according to need implies a belief in a right to a certain kind of equality. The man who is said to be in need falls below a level of benefits which is taken to be the right of all. When special provision is made for him, this is an attempt to bring him, so far as possible, up to the level of what is due equally to all. In so far as the initial lack is the result of natural causes (e.g. physical handicap), the principle of justice which attempts to remove it goes against nature. In so far as the lack is the result of established social conditions, the principle of justice goes against tradition. This principle of justice therefore may certainly be called prosthetic.

The belief in a right to equality, of which the principle of distribution according to need is one manifestation, seems to me to be fundamentally a respect for individual persons—in Kantian language, a respect for ends-in-themselves. When individuals are regarded as having a right to equality, or as being of equal worth, this does not imply an overlooking of the ways in which they are clearly of unequal worth. What I have said about merit shows that the rating of individuals on a scale of worth refers almost wholly to their utility. The Kantian principle, that we should treat all human beings as ends-in-themselves and not *merely* as means, does not say that we may not treat them as means at all. We continually treat men as means without necessarily being immoral. It is when regarded as means that men can be counted better or worse, more or less useful. But means to what? Means to the ends of others, of society, or of humanity at large. The ends to which they are a means are themselves the ends or purposes of human beings. And when it is said that men should be treated as ends-in-themselves, the meaning is that the ends of men are that by reference to which means are counted as means. Now means to an end, or a set of ends, can be rated on a scale as more or less useful for securing the end or ends. But the ends for which these means are useful cannot be placed on the same scale, precisely because they are not means but the ends themselves which provide the point of reference for rating means. The *equality* of men as ends is therefore the absence of that inequality which is correctly attached to them when they are considered as means.

JUSTICE AND UTILITY

I am saying that the principle of egalitarian justice is at root the same as Kant's categorical imperative, i.e. the basic principle of morality. Now utility is not justice; utility is a means to the end of morality. The classical utilitarians said that this end was happiness, but I think they did not go far enough. Happiness is valued because it is an end of persons; it depends on the Kantian principle.

It will be recalled that there were residual elements in the idea of merit that did not seem to be matters of utility. The development of talent and the exercise of virtue are valued not only for utility but also because they express the realization of persons both as individuals and as forming a human community. These residual elements I should count as elements of justice, and I should say that they, like the principle of equality, express the basic notion of the value of persons.

The same goes for conservative justice. The conservation of an established system of rights has a similar twofold value. In so far as it prevents the breakdown of society, it is useful. In so far as it respects rights, as being ends of persons, it is just. The initial distinction between conservative and prosthetic justice is less fundamental than a distinction between justice proper and utility.

We may now dispose of a puzzle I raised earlier, whether reward and punishment should be assigned to conservative justice, as is implied by Dahrendorf for instance, or whether they should be assigned to prosthetic justice because they modify the existing order of benefits and burdens. If the distinction between justice and utility is more fundamental than that between conservative and prosthetic justice, it is better to ask whether reward and punishment are entirely a matter of utility (as they obviously are to a large extent anyway) or whether they also involve a residual element of justice.

I have already given my own answer to this question, and I do not expect everyone to agree with it. Whatever answer one gives, however, it is notorious that, in the early days of a society, the utilitarian aspect of punishment goes relatively unnoticed, and punishment is taken to be wholly or largely a matter of retributive justice; but in the course of time, when men reflect upon the moral basis of their institutions, the idea of retribution proper recedes and tends to be replaced by that of utility. I think the same sort of development affects the idea of the justice of reward and the principle of merit in general. It also applies to the concept of conservative justice. Primitive societies think of the established social order as fixed by nature or by supernatural beings. They think that it needs to be protected as representing a fixed order of justice, and that inroads upon that order are unjust in themselves. Later reflection leads to the view that the existing order may not be the most just, but that the conservation of its main fabric is useful, simply because it is *an* order, better than the disorder which would follow a wholesale departure from it. Nevertheless piecemeal revision is approved in the name of justice proper.

Here I revert again to Dahrendorf. He assumes, in Marxian fashion, that the revision of an existing system of social rules is always due to the revolt of an oppressed group, who suffer from the sanctions of the existing order. He presumably thinks (or so it appears) that all groups act from motives of self-interest, the upper classes wishing to conserve the present order because it favours them, and the lower wishing to revise it because it oppresses them. This explains many (perhaps not all) revolutions, but fails to explain those reforms which come about from the moral sensitivity of some of the fortunate towards the distress of the unfortunate.

I find it curious that recent accounts of justice should so often rely upon a Hobbesian scheme of self-interest. Dahrendorf is not the only contributor to *Philosophy, Politics and Society, Second Series*, to take this line. It is also taken by Professor John Rawls in his article 'Justice as Fairness'. Rawls makes it clear that he is not presupposing, like the usual stereotype of Hobbes, that men's *only* motive is self-interest. But his account of justice as fairness relies upon a notion of quasi-contract which comes about from thoughts of 'mutual self-interest'. Most oddly of all, Professor A. M. Honoré, in an article on 'Social Justice' (*McGill Law Journal*,

February 1962), again uses a Hobbesian hypothesis to account for the notion of justice. I say most oddly of all, because Honoré, like myself, interprets the concept of social justice as basically equalitarian. In order to account for this equalitarianism, he refers to Hobbes's view of men as roughly equal to power and therefore in fear of each other. I have the greatest respect for Hobbes, and it would be absurd to deny the force of what he says about human equality. Nevertheless it simply will not do to base equalitarian *justice* on men's natural powers and fear of each other. These Hobbesian facts imply that one can risk exerting one's power against another where one sees that the other is abnormally weak. So indeed one can. But the sentiment of justice urges precisely the opposite course of action. It urges us to give special consideration to the weak or the needy, from whom we have little to fear. If the fortunate fear the *numbers* of the needy, and meet their demands on that account, they have not been motivated to do so by thoughts of *justice*.

Hobbesian facts account well enough for conservative justice and for the so-called justice, but really utility, of distribution according to merit. Prosthetic justice proper, which asserts a universal right to equality especially manifest in the claims of need, must depend on non-egoistic sentiments.

Someone may say this is all very well, but I am obscuring the distinction between justice and generosity or charity. In fact, it may be said, the whole business of altruistic provision for need, which I have stressed, is a matter of generosity or charity, not of justice at all. It is indeed moral action at its best, but that is not justice. In identifying the basic principle of justice with Kant's categorical imperative, am I not making justice the whole of morality, including generosity?

I think not. My view is that charity turns into justice when the needs of the beneficiaries are widely recognized in a society as moral *claims*. No one has a right to charity, but once the benefit which the needy lack is regarded as something due to all, as something to which all have a right, it passes out of the domain of charity into that of justice. Would anyone say that the Welfare State is a *charity* organization, or deny that it is a more *just* (whether or not it be judged a better) society than one in which the relief of basic needs is left to private generosity? Would anyone say that the provision of uneconomic transport services to remote, sparsely populated areas of Britain is charitable rather than fair? Conservative justice preserves established rights. Prosthetic justice adds further rights, rights to benefits which were not formerly counted due as a matter of right. In this way, with the development of the social conscience (and of the economic capacity of a society), the field of justice gradually takes in more from the field of charity. The character of the order of rights to be protected by conservative justice accordingly changes, the society becomes a more just society, and the nature of justice itself, both conservative and prosthetic, becomes clearer.

G

6 Chaim Perelman on Justice

Professor Chaim Perelman's long essay *De la justice*, first published in 1945, is a powerful piece of writing which has had a wide influence. For these reasons it should long continue to be read and critically examined, although Perelman himself may consider some aspects of it to have been superseded by his later publications. For example, the English translation which appeared in 1963 under the title 'Concerning Justice'[1] includes a footnote[2] which seems to imply a modification of the view that values are 'logically arbitrary'. The footnote says that, since writing these remarks about values in the essay on justice, Perelman 'has tried to present, through his theory of argumentation, a way of reasoning about values'. This suggests that his later account of argumentation qualifies the earlier bare statement that values are arbitrary. Nevertheless, even in the original form of the essay on justice, there is a clear link with Perelman's views on logic and rhetoric, for his distinction between formal and concrete justice is a vivid illustration of the difference that he sees between the reasoning of formal logic and the kind of debate which goes on in the area of rhetoric.

It is notorious that differences of opinion about justice, both among philosophers and among practising politicians, are sharper than such differences on most other values. Perelman's essay does not aim at ending controversy; on the contrary, it insists on recognizing that there must always be controversy about basic social values. Its intention is rather to clarify the character of the controversy and to narrow its scope by distinguishing what is necessarily incontrovertible from what is necessarily controvertible. Having first listed a number of different suggested principles of justice, each of which appears to have some solidity, Perelman argues that all of them conform to what he calls the principle of formal justice. This is the principle that 'beings of one and the same essential category must be treated in the same way'. The differences arise over what is to constitute 'the essential category'.

There is no doubt that this notion of a principle of formal justice, common to all the conflicting conceptions of justice, has made an important contribution to philosophical understanding, and it has been adopted (if not always precisely in Perelman's terms) in various later treatments of the subject. Perelman points out that there can be no controversy about formal justice simply because it is purely formal and abstract. If you leave aside the question of what counts as the essential category to qualify for identical treatment, nobody can question the precept that all members of this one category should be treated alike. If they all belong to the same category, and if that category is essential for the purpose in hand, there cannot be any reason to differentiate between them. It is obviously rational to treat them alike.

The acceptance of such rationality, according to Perelman, is a consequence of our tendency to inertia,[3] a prime example being the juridical practice of conforming to precedent. Formal rationality, on this account, depends on the universality (or near-universality) of a psychological trait analogous to the universal law of inertia that governs the behaviour of all physical bodies. Such a universal causal agency is to be contrasted with the particular causes constituted by social conditions in different milieux, which will lead to different conceptions of concrete justice. One cannot expect to find universal acceptance of the rationality of any such conception, since the rationality in this case does not depend on a psychological trait common to all mankind. Individual history and experience of specific social conditions are the causal influences on judgement about the principle of concrete justice, on whether moral merit, or hard work, or rank, or need, is the proper criterion for a 'just' distribution. So any argument in favour of one of these conceptions must take account of the different susceptibilities of different audiences; it must conform to the principles of rhetoric, not to those of formal logic.

This is an interesting thesis, with a good deal of persuasiveness about it. Perelman's main distinction between formal and concrete justice seems to me very valuable. It is certainly true that his principle of formal justice has a rationality which is incontrovertible, a universality independent of particular feelings engendered by particular conditions. We must likewise acknowledge that the various principles of concrete justice present a wholly different picture. What seems rational to one group is sheer prejudice in the eyes of another. Very often (though not always) a man's predilection for a particular conception depends on his personal history; people who have experienced or seen at close quarters the grinding evil of poverty will generally say that justice should have regard to needs, while people who have seen the beneficial social effects of hard work and the appalling consequences of idleness will at least add that justice should look to merit.

Nevertheless I want to suggest that Perelman's distinction between formal and concrete justice is too sharp. I think that Perelman exaggerates the arbitrary character of the values which lie behind different conceptions of concrete justice. One can show rational connections between some of them so as to reduce the number of competing principles; and although a genuine conflict remains, I believe that there is more rationality to it than Perelman appears to allow. This leads me to a final comment about the relation between rational justification and causal explanation.

ii

Perelman gives a list of six popular principles of justice:[4]
1. To each the same thing.
2. To each according to his merits.
3. To each according to his works.
4. To each according to his needs.
5. To each according to his rank.
6. To each according to his legal entitlement.

Perelman points out[5] that the first of these can be regarded as simply a version of the principle of formal justice, but less clear than his own version because it does not show the principle of formal justice to be a generic one common to all proposed principles of concrete justice. That seems very reasonable. But Perelman then goes on to treat all the other five principles in his list as each having much the same sort of logical relationship to the principle of formal justice. That is to say, he regards merit, work, need, rank, and legal entitlement as being each an independent value (in the mathematical sense—but also in the ethical sense) for the variable 'the same essential category'. According to the doctrine of the essay 'Concerning Justice', each of these values is chosen arbitrarily by those who make it the essential category for justice.

It seems to me that principles 2–6 are not all simple alternatives to each other, and that the adoption of certain of them is not a matter of arbitrary choice.

First of all, principle 6 is quite different from all the rest, as indeed Perelman himself recognizes[6] from the point of view of the person judging. Principle 6 is concerned with the retention of the *status quo* of rights, while all the rest contemplate a distribution of new rights or a redistribution of old ones. Elsewhere[7] I have distinguished between conservative and reforming aspects of the concept of justice. Principle 6 belongs to the conservative aspect. Whatever principle or principles of reformative justice people may accept, most of them will *also* accept principle 6 as a necessary principle of conservative justice. Everyone who agrees that a society needs laws will agree that the rights conferred by those laws ought to be maintained. The only people who will reject principle 6 are anarchists, and they will reject it simply because they reject the need for a State and law.

The difference of opinion between anarchists and non-anarchists does not depend on any difference in values; it depends on their different judgements of facts. The values of the anarchist are the values of the liberal: individual liberty, self-determination, voluntary co-operation. The question at issue between the anarchist and the non-anarchist is the practical possibility of giving effect to liberal values without having a State. It is true that a State and its law imply some limitation on individual liberty, but in a democratic State this is in order to achieve a maximum of liberty for all. The opponent of anarchism believes that without the constraints of law and State there will be less liberty overall because of the deficiencies of human nature. His dispute with the anarchist is about psychological facts, not about values.

Apart from anarchists, then, everyone will accept principle 6 as *a* necessary principle of (conservative) justice. This does not exclude the acceptance, in addition, of one or more principles of reformative justice. But of course it also does not require the acceptance of any such additional principle. It is possible to hold principle 6 as the *only* principle of justice, as meaning that each person should receive his legal entitlement and nothing more. Such a view may be taken by arch-conservatives, believing that the idea of justice relates only to the maintenance of the *status quo*.

At first sight, one is inclined to say that the difference of opinion between them and those who think of justice as also a reformative concept is a difference in value-judgement. But I am not sure that this is correct. If one wanted to argue with an arch-conservative, it would not be very effective to do so by invoking sympathy for the underprivileged. The arch-conservative could reply: 'Of course I sympathize with these people. Of course I agree that it is a good action, perhaps even a duty, to help them. What I deny is that it is a matter of justice. The value involved is a matter of charity or benevolence, not of justice.' In order to change his opinion, you need to alter his conception of the meaning and implications of justice, rather than to persuade him to accept a value which he does not now accept. You might try to do it by pointing out to him that no system of law is static and no society is static. As society changes, law needs to change. In order to decide what changes should be made in the law, one must have non-legal criteria for judging what new laws should be made and what old laws should be repealed. Thus there must be some principle or principles for reforming the law. Some of these reformative principles, designed to affect law, are commonly called principles of fairness or equity or 'natural justice', and if they are necessary there is no reason to deny them the name of principles of justice. At any rate, this seems a possible way of arguing with the arch-conservative and trying to persuade him to widen his concept of justice. As before, the difference of opinion does not really rest on the holding of different values. The argument points to facts, this time to sociological facts.

I turn now to the remaining principles in Perelman's list, distribution according to merit, work, need, or rank. There is an affinity between distribution according to merit and distribution according to work or rank; if taken as essential categories for distributive justice, work and rank are dependent upon the more general category of merit. This can be seen more easily if we substitute for 'merit' the term 'worth', which Aristotle uses in his formulation of distributive justice. The concept of worth includes not only moral merit but also talent. Aristotle's example is that flutes should be given to those with a talent for flute-playing. Talent is a species of worth. Effort, whether in the form of moral effort or of hard work, is a species of worth. Rank or status is counted as a species of worth. The principle that it is just to distribute benefits or responsibilities according to worth can be interpreted so as to include the recognition of talent, moral merit, work, and rank.

The valuing of all these different species of worth as relevant for just distribution is not an arbitrary matter; it depends largely on the thought of utility. If flutes are in short supply, the most efficient use of them is to give them to people who can make pleasing music with them. If facilities for higher education are limited, society will benefit most by giving those facilities to people who have the talents that can be developed by higher education. The actions which are called morally virtuous are commonly useful to society and this is at least a main reason why they are commended; the reward of moral virtue is itself useful because it encourages such virtue. Hard work is likewise commended because of its social utility, and the justice of rewarding such effort depends on the utility of encouraging it. The utilitarian foundation in this instance is especially clear from the fact that nobody would think it proper to reward work which is pointless or socially harmful. As for the valuation of rank, this depends on the idea that rank was originally bestowed as a reward for valuable service to the community (or perhaps, in the case of hereditary monarchy, as the recognition of talent for the office); and in periods when people have thought it just to distribute benefits and responsibilities according to rank, they did so because they supposed that the useful qualities which had earned the rank were transmitted by heredity.

If the justice of distribution according to worth depends on the thought of utility, then utility can also supply a rational criterion for judging between competing claims of the different kinds of worth. For example, if we have to choose between distribution according to work and distribution according to rank, it is rational to prefer the one which will be obviously useful to the one which is doubtfully so. It is less easy to decide between work and talent or between either of these and moral merit, but in principle we have a criterion for judgement. While our personal preferences have no doubt been heavily influenced by the psychological effects of individual circumstances, the comparison of these different values is not arbitrary, nor are the values themselves independent of each other.

I should add, however, that the justice of distribution according to worth does not depend *entirely* on the thought of social utility. When we value talent and the provision for its development, we are not thinking *only* of social utility; we are thinking also of the self-realization of the individual concerned. A flute for the flute-player will give pleasure to the public who hear him; but it also gives enormous satisfaction to the flute-player himself, and surely this is part of what we have in mind when we decide to spend public money on scholarships for young people with a talent for playing the flute. Public provision for education of all kinds depends in part on the social utility of developing talents and in part on the valuing of self-development for its own sake. There is a similar duality in our valuation of moral merit. The moral virtues are socially useful and are valued largely for that reason; but they are also valued as an essential part of self-realization as a human being. I doubt whether the same thing applies to work as such (though some people would say it does), and I do not believe for a moment that it applies to rank.

The principle of distribution according to need is quite different from all these variations on the theme of distribution according to worth. You cannot regard need as a species of worth in the way that talent, moral merit, work, and rank are all species of worth. We do not commend or value need as we commend or value talent, merit, and work. Need in itself is an evil, not a good; something to be removed, not something to be fostered. Distribution according to needs has nothing to do with deserts; if we regard needs, we must treat deserts as irrelevant. The really serious conflicts in the application of justice are precisely those in which we have to choose between needs and deserts—or, looking at it in a different light, between needs and social utility. A good deal of the differences in social policy between socialists and conservatives depends on the relative emphasis which they give to the conflicting principles of justice, the one regarding needs, the other regarding worth or social utility.

The meeting of needs is not entirely independent of social utility. The slave-owner, who valued his slave solely for utility, would meet the slave's need for food and health in order that the slave could go on working. Marx's analysis of capitalism assumes that employers generally take the same attitude towards their workers.

And certainly it is true that the maintenance of life and health in the working population of a society is necessary for the continuance of their work, and so is socially useful. But what about the non-working section of the population? In the case of the children, there is the future to be thought of; children must be kept alive and well now, if they are to make their contribution when they are grown up. The same can be said of the curably sick; although they cannot work at present, they will be able to contribute once more to society if they are cared for and helped to recover. There remain the old and the incurably sick. They are no longer able to contribute to the welfare of society. From the point of view of social utility, there is no reason to meet their needs. So the claim of justice in their case cannot be based on the thought of utility. What is more, although the desirability of meeting needs in other cases *can* be based on utility, this is surely not what we have in mind when we think of the claim of need as a claim of *justice*. So far as the claim of need is concerned, there is no difference between those who can contribute to society and those who cannot. That is why Marx's condemnation of the capitalist attitude is so effective; in his picture of them, the capitalists, like the slave-owners, think only of the use-value of the workers and pay no regard to their needs as human beings. The principle of justice which looks to need depends on the valuation of individual human beings for their own sakes. In Kantian language, it regards them as ends-in-themselves.

The next thing to observe is that the needs principle of justice has an affinity with the equalitarian principle. While Perelman is quite right to point to similarities between some versions of an equality principle and his own principle of formal justice, equalitarians in practice have been concerned with something more substantial. Where meritarians pay chief attention to those differences among human beings that are relevant to utility—differences of capacity and effort—equalitarians pay chief attention to the things that all human beings have in common. The principle of distribution according to need has been supported by equalitarians as a principle of levelling up. Different people differ in their needs, and so distribution according to need is a differentiated form of distribution; those in greater need receive more, those in lesser need receive less. At first sight, therefore, the needs principle seems similar to the worth principle, which also gives more to some and less to others. But the end result of a needs distribution is to reduce inequality, while the end result of a worth distribution is to increase inequality. If the man with greater needs is given more than the man with lesser needs, the intended result is that each of them should have (or at least approach) the same level of satisfaction; the inequality of nature is corrected. But if the man of greater talent or greater industry is rewarded more than the man of lesser talent or industry, the pre-existing inequality between them is increased; for the man of greater talent or industry is in any case likely to achieve greater satisfactions for himself by his own efforts, and if he is rewarded in addition he will be better off still.

In my view, therefore, the first five of the popular principles of justice in Perelman's list should be classified into two groups. On the one side the principles of merit, work, and rank go together; on the other side the equalitarian principle and the principle of need. The former group depends largely on the valuation of social utility, the latter group depends on the valuation of all human beings as ends-in-themselves. I have noted, however, that some aspects of the first group do not depend entirely on the thought of social utility but also take account of the value of individual self-realization. The latter value is an aspect of the Kantian idea that each human being is an end-in-himself.

The Kantian notion is itself not free from internal conflict, for we often have to weigh up the claims of one individual human being (or one group of them) against the claims of another. Nevertheless it seems to me that many of the most serious conflicts of values in *social* life, many of the serious differences of value-judgement in different ideologies, boil down to a conflict between the claims of the general interest and the claims of the individual—in philosophical terms, between utilitarian ethics and Kantian ethics. I have no formula, of universal acceptability, for resolving this fundamental conflict. But the analysis which I have presented does introduce a greater element of rationality into principles of justice than does Perelman's account.

iii

My final comment concerns Perelman's theory of argumentation. As I mentioned in expounding Perelman's view, he regards rationality as a matter of acceptability to audiences. The rationality of formal justice is acceptable to a universal audience and depends upon the universal, or near-universal, character of a psychological trait of inertia. Perelman thinks this is illustrated by the juridical practice of following precedent. In his view, the practice seems rational simply because our habit of inertia leads us naturally to react in the same way to a repetition of the same circumstances.

Such an account implies that rational justification is to be understood in terms of causal explanation; it implies that the psychological origin of a practice is fundamentally identical with the sufficient reason for continuing the practice. Likewise, if I have not misunderstood him, Perelman holds that the more limited rationality of rhetorical argumentation is to be understood in terms of sociology; a conclusion can appear rational to a particular audience because it appeals to a value which just happens, as a contingent sociological fact, to be accepted by that particular audience.

It seems to me that this identification of rational justification with causal explanation is not borne out by the examples with which I have been concerned in this essay. Let us take first Perelman's own illustration of the rationality of formal justice, namely the juridical practice of following precedent. This may well owe its origin to the psychological trait of inertia, and perhaps inertia is also the cause of our feeling that the practice is 'just' or 'fair'. But when courts and jurists give *reasons* for the principle of *stare decisis*, they do not refer to this general feeling or to a psychological reluctance to innovate. Their reasons are firmly utilitarian. The practice of following precedent is defended on the ground of 'certainty', i.e. of enabling lawyers to predict, in cases without novel features, what a court would decide, and so to advise their clients with confidence. Certainly in the United Kingdom it is taken for granted that this is the rationale of following precedent. Confirmation may be found in two recent *dicta* of the House of Lords (the final court of appeal). One was in a Practice Statement of 1966,[8] announcing that the House of Lords would not in future necessarily be bound by its own past decisions. The other was in a judgement of 1978,[9] in which the House of Lords insisted that the Court of Appeal (i.e. the court immediately below the House of Lords) should be bound by that court's own past decisions. When a higher court, such as the British House of Lords, finds it necessary to give reasons for the practice of *stare decisis*, it is because, in a particular case, the practice has appeared to *conflict* with sentiments of justice or fairness, and the issue for the higher court has been one of weighing up the general utility of the practice of following precedent against the apparent injustice of applying it in a particular case.

Again, my discussion of the different principles of concrete justice has shown that the appeal of each of them does not rest on a specific value which is accepted by some particular audience and not by others. If the principle of distribution according to rank were taken to be independent of all the others, it would appear to confirm Perelman's view. For support of this principle of justice is confined to particular societies over a limited period of time; there is virtually no support for it in modern societies. But once we see that its rationale depends on the wider concept of merit or worth, we can no longer say that rational argumentation about it depends entirely on sociological conditions. We can argue about the respective claims of the principles of rank, merit, work, and talents in terms of their common subordination to the concept of social utility, a value of universal acceptability.

The same thing can be said, with some qualification, about the Kantian value which underlies the equalitarian and the needs concept of justice, and which partly sustains the principles of moral merit and talents. Of course it is not true to say that all societies have in fact accepted the Kantian idea that all human beings are ends-in-themselves. But, unlike the more restricted principles of value which many societies have in fact followed, the Kantian principle is by its very nature universal in application and in appeal. A principle which gives value to all human beings can be valued by all human beings. At any rate, the rationality of an argument which depends on the Kantian principle cannot be called particularistic.

It remains true that conflicts are apt to arise between the principle of utility and the principle of valuing individuals as ends-in-themselves—and indeed within the latter principle alone, when a choice has to be made between serving the ends of different individuals. The universality of the two principles is no guarantee against having to face moral dilemmas. The process of deliberation which we undertake in such circumstances may well conform more to

Perelman's picture of rhetorical argumentation. It is easy to think of conflicts of values in which different decisions would seem right to an average West European democrat and an average East European communist (to say nothing of the views of Chinese, or Indians, or West Africans, or whatever). I should not want to claim that there is some form of universally acceptable reasoning which would yield a single right answer, and I am therefore ready to follow Perelman in his view that the rationality of deliberation in such moral dilemmas cannot go beyond sociological factors. Nevertheless it seems to me that, even in the realm of values, there is wider scope for universal rationality than Perelman has allowed.

7 John Rawls's Theory of Justice

i

In several articles published over a period of ten years Professor John Rawls outlined a distinctive account of justice together with certain implications of his approach. It was clear from the articles that he had something important to say, but it was not clear precisely what. Some philosophical insights perhaps cannot of their very nature be made plain. This did not seem to be true of Rawls's thesis. He was writing in and of a tradition of moral philosophy in the English language which has been unusually lucid, and he obviously possessed a powerful analytic intelligence. It was frustrating to find that a man who had learned so much from Henry Sidgwick fell so far short of Sidgwick in clarity of expression.

The first part of Rawls's book, *A Theory of Justice* (1971 and 1972), gives one some hope that the frustration will be removed. These chapters are certainly clearer than the articles from which they grew. They also suggest that Rawls has learned from the criticisms of others and has modified his view to meet the criticisms. All students of philosophy profess themselves ready to learn from criticism, but few of us are modest enough or pliant enough to get far with it in practice. One admires a man who has patiently added to and adjusted the structure of his theory in the light of critical comment over some fourteen years before allowing his projected book to see the light of day. Everybody who has read Rawls's articles will have expected the book to be an important one, and so indeed it is.

Yet despite (perhaps partly because of) its great length, its value does not match the expectations of readers or the abilities of the author. There is an increase of clarity in places, but elsewhere ambiguity and loose ends remain. The latter half of the book relapses not so much into obscurity as into vagueness. Reiterated assertion takes the place of argument, and sometimes Rawls's undertaking to meet a criticism is only half fulfilled. When he uses mathematical diagrams Rawls can be wonderfully clear in explaining a principle or the difference between alternative possibilities. When it comes to words he is often fluffy. An elaborate (non-mathematical) diagram on p. 109 gives the impression that he has fully worked out in his mind a complete scheme of concepts of practical reason and their mutual relations. Yet time and time again in the course of reading the book one feels that he has not really decided where he stands on relationships that should be basic to his plan, e.g. between the concept of right (adjective) and that of justice. The lack of rigour in so much of the book may be simply a failure of expression, but at times it looks like a failure to think things through.

There are three main areas of discussion for moral philosophy: first, logical questions about the meaning and function of moral concepts; second, criteriological questions about the standard or standards in fact used, or recommended for use, in deciding what one ought to do; and third, metaphysical questions about the presuppositions of moral thinking and their consistency or inconsistency with the presuppositions of other well-established modes of thought. Rawls's book is not concerned at all with the third of these and only marginally with the first. It is almost entirely devoted to the second, but in greater detail than usual and with attention to a range of implications, especially for economic theory and to a limited extent for political philosophy and for moral psychology.

The second area of discussion may fairly be regarded as the most important one in the history of moral philosophy. In the latter part of that history, the dominant theory, certainly among writers in the English language, has been utilitarianism. Rawls finds utilitarianism unsatisfactory and seeks an alternative. The most popular alternative historically, Rawls says, has been intuitionism. (He also discusses 'perfectionism' as a third possibility but evidently feels, correctly in my opinion, that this is not really in the running as compared with utilitarianism and intuitionism.) By 'intuitionism' Rawls means any theory which holds that there is a plurality of basic principles of right action. Intuitionism suffers from two defects. First, it is unable to explain why its principles should be followed; they just have to be accepted as fundamental moral 'intuitions'. Second, it gives no guidance for decision when two or more of its principles point to conflicting courses of action in a particular situation. These are familiar objections. Most utilitarians (but not Sidgwick, and of course not the so-called 'ideal utilitarians', H. Rashdall and G. E. Moore) base the principles of moral action on factors in human psychology (desires and feelings), and most of them again (with Sidgwick once more the outstanding exception) offer the principle of utility as a single fundamental principle that forms the justification for secondary principles and is therefore the criterion for resolving conflicts between secondary principles in any particular situation. But if utilitarianism has its own difficulties, is there some other way of meeting the objections that face intuitionism?

Rawls's originality lies in giving a novel answer to this question. In his preface he disclaims originality, saying that his theory is 'highly Kantian in nature', but this is false modesty. It would indeed be a *sounder* theory, in my opinion, if it deviated less from Kant, but that is a different matter.

ii

Rawls deals with the first defect of intuitionism by proposing a contractual hypothesis as a method of arriving at principles of justice without having to rely simply on intuition. If that could be done successfully, it would be a great gain. Not only would it explain what intuitionism leaves unexplained. It would also resolve a material disagreement, for there is no consensus on the substance of the principles of justice, as there is on many other common principles of morality. As things are, one large group of people stands pat on the intuition that justice requires distribution according to merit, while another large group insists on an alternative (or additional) principle of distribution, something regarded as based on simple equality, sometimes as based on need. Rawls sides with the second group and thinks that his contractual hypothesis leads to that conclusion. The hypothesis is supposed to avoid a recourse to intuition because it depends on a judgement of prudence instead of morality.

Rawls's point is that a judgement of fairness coincides with a particular kind of judgement of prudence. He imagines men in an initial position of equality. They have knowledge of the general laws of psychology and the social sciences, but they are ignorant of particular facts both about themselves and about the society in which they live. They are conceived to be self-interested and rational (i.e. disposed to choose the most efficient means to predetermined ends, the relevant end here being their own maximum advantage). In coming together to form a society they must agree on principles for the distribution of benefits and burdens. What are the principles on which such people would agree? According to Rawls, they would insist first on a form of equality. Secondly, they would require any departure from equality to benefit everyone, and especially those who are least advantaged. When introducing the notion on p. 14 Rawls says that the first principle 'requires equality in the assignment of basic rights and duties'. Later (especially pp. 60, 302) he is more specific, confining the first principle to liberty, which he regards as the most basic of rights. Each of the hypothetical contractors, Rawls believes, would think that the combination of these two principles offers the best chance of maximum advantage. Each is ignorant of particular facts and so does not know whether he will be well or ill endowed and placed as compared with his fellows. For all he knows, he may be among the least advantaged. Therefore he will choose a scheme that does the best possible for everyone, and especially for the least advantaged. Such a scheme need not be, indeed is unlikely to be, completely equalitarian; for a non-equalitarian plan that gives $x+1$ units of good to the least advantaged makes them better off than does an equalitarian plan that gives x units to everyone. This is why the second principle is added to the strictly equalitarian first principle.

The hypothesis does not state the meaning of justice or fairness. When the man on the Clapham omnibus says something is just or fair, he clearly does not mean that it is in accordance with principles that would be chosen by rational persons, making a social contract in order to maximize their individual interests, in circumstances in which they knew lots of general truths but were ignorant of particular facts. Rawls does not suppose this. He tells us what would be judged *prudent* in the hypothetical circumstances, and his view is that this coincides in *content* with what we normally judge to be just. On p. 111 Rawls says that the kind of account he has given is an 'explication', not 'an analysis of the meaning of the term "right" as normally used in moral contexts'. (I think he would

H

apply the remark to 'just' as well as to 'right', for he talks later on the same page of 'the theory of justice as fairness, or more generally of rightness as fairness'.) But he goes on to declare that the explication is an 'analysis' or 'definition' in the sense that it provides a satisfactory substitute for a troublesome expression and thereby enables us to eliminate that expression. I take it this is consistent with what I have said above. Rawls's account does not tell us what we mean by saying that something is just, but it is an alternative method of lighting on the same something with intellectual satisfaction if we are puzzled by the notion of justice. We can say it is what prudence would recommend to us in the hypothetical circumstances of Rawls's contract. Since one of the circumstances (the 'veil of ignorance' about particular facts, especially concerning oneself) makes the same choice prudent for everyone, the prudential judgement takes on a universality, an impersonality, that we do not ordinarily associate with prudence. This is why it can be a substitute for the impartial judgement of what is just, fair for all. Lots of philosophers have tried to substitute a judgement of prudence for one of morality. A simple substitution is unsatisfactory because the two things are plainly different. Hume pinpointed one of the essential differences: 'the language of morals' differs from 'the language of self-love' in taking a universal point of view. Rawls's hypothesis is a means of conferring a universal point of view on the prudential outlook.

Unfortunately it does not lead necessarily to his particular conclusions. The point has been made by other critics and need not be laboured. Why should the contractors make liberty their basic good? They would if they had been educated in the U.S.A., but probably not if in the Soviet Union or China. Well, can we try to abstract from the effect of education? Rawls's contractors are supposed to be ignorant of the stage of civilization that their society has reached. For all they know, they might find themselves in the affluence of modern America or in the famine of Egypt at the time of Joseph. In the latter event they would put bread before freedom (cf. Genesis 47: 19). If their choice as contractors is to be prepared for all eventualities, should they not make the means of subsistence their basic good?

This is on the assumption that it is the part of prudence to prepare for the worst, an assumption that Rawls in fact makes. But we may also ask, why is it necessarily rational to play safe rather than gamble a little (cf. Michael Lessnoff, *Political Studies*, March 1971, p. 76)? Rawls supposes that a rational man, moved by self-interest and not knowing whether he will be among the lucky ones or the unlucky, will prefer to maximize the good of the latter than to offer glittering prizes for the former. But what about a middle course, a sort of Welfare State, in which the unlucky are guaranteed a bare subsistence while the lucky can go for not so glittering but still quite attractive prizes? Is it clearly rational to put that aside? There is a chance after all that one will end up among the lucky people; and even if one does not, there is, as Adam Smith said, a vicarious satisfaction to be obtained from contemplating the pleasures of 'the rich and the great', especially since Rawls's contractors are supposed to lack envy.

Rawls's hypothesis does not provide a method of deciding between rival conceptions of justice. It is tailored to fit one of these, but can be stretched to cover another; and we are given no reason why it should not be differently tailored anyway. Rawls favours a conception of justice that leans towards equalitarianism and distribution according to need. He criticizes the view that the proper principle is distribution according to merit. He supposes that his hypothesis leads to his own conception. But, as we have seen, it is possible to say that his rational contractors would choose a system that included prizes for those who are gifted or otherwise fortunate. It is not only possible, but plausible, to argue that his rational contractors would positively prefer a system of distribution strictly according to merit. For merit proper does not depend on the luck of the game but on a man's effort to do the best he can with the abilities and circumstances that fall to his lot. The initial contractor does not know what his individual abilities and circumstances will be, compared with those of other people. He does know (it is part of his supposed knowledge of general principles) that it is equally within everyone's power to use, or fail to use, to the full such abilities and opportunities as he will have. Since *this* depends, not on chance, but on his own choice, a rational man will plump for a system that distributes advantage according to merit. (Rawls says on p. 310 that the principle of distribution according to desert 'would not be chosen in the original position', but his argument is perfunctory and to my mind quite unconvincing.)

Then again, Rawls adds to his hypothesis the proviso that his initial contractors lack envy. This is to avoid their choosing a strictly equalitarian system in which the level of goods, for each as well as for all, is less than it might be. Rawls is ready to accept inequality provided that it means increased benefit for all groups including the poorest. Someone who thinks that justice (as contrasted with some other principle of morality) insists on strict equality, could still use Rawls's hypothesis but without depriving the contractors of envy, in which case they could be supposed to go for a bare equalitarianism.

Strictly speaking, Rawls's hypothesis is not coherent. It does not really make sense to suppose that people might know the general laws of psychology and the social sciences while being unacquainted with any individual facts about their own abilities and the character of their own society. The sciences in question are empirical, not *a priori* like pure mathematics, so an understanding of them depends on acquaintance with individual facts of the kind on which the general laws are based; and if a hypothetical person were debarred from having experiential knowledge of his own abilities and his own society, then he could not have experiential, or derived, knowledge of *anyone's* abilities or *any* society. Even if this objection were invalid, it would still be true that the general knowledge postulated by Rawls would be so thin as to be useless. Since the contractors are ignorant of the stage of civilization of their society, the 'laws' of psychology, economics, and politics that they know must be such as would apply equally to tribal as to industrial society. A difference in form of society often means a difference of psychology as well as of social institutions, and the sort of psychological and economic 'laws' that apply throughout the whole gamut would tell one virtually nothing about predictable behaviour.

Perhaps this insistence on strict coherence is misplaced. A tale of fantasy is similarly incoherent if details are pressed; yet we can understand it on the superficial level intended by the author, and can see its point. A philosophical hypothesis like that of Rawls is admittedly fantastic but can be intelligible and have point. In one place (p. 449) Rawls compares his hypothesis with the more realistic situation of 'delegates to a constitutional convention, and ideal legislators and voters', where similar though less strict limitations apply. A legislator has to frame policies for the future, relying on knowledge of general facts and ignorant of the way in which they will work out in detail for individual cases. That is to say, the principles of morals include the principles of legislation. Nevertheless, as my implicit reference to Bentham should recall, legislators do not judge simply in terms of prudence. Bentham's theory supposes the private individual to be motivated by self-interest and the legislator to be motivated by benevolence. Of course that is an idealization (cf. Rawls's reference to 'ideal' legislators and voters), but it is not a fantasy, and it is a way of making the point that the standard of right action, as utilitarians understand it, coincides with the choice that legislators *would* make it they acted purely from benevolence. It explains the judgement of right by describing a hypothetical fact, just as Rawls tries to do. The relevance of Bentham's hypothesis is obvious. There is no need to elaborate a fantasy when a genuine analogy is at hand.

iii

The purpose of Rawls's hypothesis is to eliminate intuition. It does not in fact do so, for reasons that I have already given. The details of the hypothesis are manipulated so as to yield a preconceived view, i.e. a particular moral intuition; and even then the hypothesis does not necessarily lead to Rawls's conclusions, which are thus shown again to rest on intuition. Now Rawls knows very well that there is an alternative method of trying to dispense with intuition, the method followed by empiricist moral philosophers, including some of the leading utilitarians. It is to base moral judgement on factors of moral and social psychology, and notably on sympathy. Rawls rejects the concept of a sympathetic spectator for this purpose. He takes it to be a device of utilitarian theory for thinking of the interests of society as if they were the interests of a single individual, and he says the trouble with utilitarianism is that 'it does not take seriously the distinction between persons' (pp. 27, 187). One can reasonably complain of utilitarianism that it does not take the distinction seriously *enough*, but not on the ground alleged by Rawls. The concept of the sympathetic spectator, as used by classical theorists, does not blur the distinction between persons. This is true even of Hume, who did found utility on sympathy. It is more obviously true of Adam Smith, who developed the notion of the sympathetic spectator in order to *oppose* utilitarianism and to support an empiricist version of natural law theory.

If one adopts the empiricist method of founding moral judgement on sympathy and other psychological factors, one then has to explain the logical relation between the relevant psychological facts and the normative judgements. That is to say, one needs to deal with the logic of morals as well as with the standards of right action. Rawls is led to think that he can dispense with the former task because his contractual hypothesis reduces the 'ought' of morality to that of prudence.

It is in fact not clear whether the contractual hypothesis is supposed to apply to moral judgement as a whole or only to judgements of distributive justice. Rawls says on p. 17 that his version of the contract theory is intended only to apply to justice, and that if this were found to be reasonably successful, one might (though he will not, in this book at least) go on to consider whether the idea could be extended to the more general notion of rightness and perhaps to a still wider conception of all moral relationships. Yet later he often writes as if his theory did apply to the concept of rightness in general. Indeed, if this were not the case, Rawls would not have given us an alternative to utilitarianism. The main objection to utilitarianism is that our intuitive convictions often oppose justice to utility and at times give priority to justice. Now a non-utilitarian view of justice can account for the opposition but not for the priority. For the latter purpose we need a theory of right. Utilitarianism says that the right action (both when it is and when it is not also a just action) is always the most useful action. If we want to deny that, if we want to say that sometimes the right action (being also a just action) is not the most useful, we need to show what is the criterion of rightness. This cannot be the same as the criterion of justice, for there are also times when we judge that the right action *is* the most useful one even though it is not also a just action and indeed may be an alternative to the just action. For example, in time of war the most useful method of selecting men for military service or demobilization is not the fairest method, as we ordinarily conceive of fairness; yet most people would agree that it is right in those circumstances for the national interest to prevail over fairness. Rawls would probably say that his theory allows a decision to follow utility in such a situation, provided that the useful result will benefit people in all positions and especially the most needy. If so, he is regarding his theory as one of rightness, not of justice or fairness as commonly understood.

This brings me to the second part of Rawls's originality, his method of dealing with a conflict between principles. He calls this the priority problem, i.e. the problem of deciding which moral principle should have priority in a situation of conflict. The weakness of intuitionism is especially striking here, for the intuition to which it appeals is different from the intuition of principles. The intuition of principles is commonly held to be a rational understanding of what is necessary and universal, comparable with the understanding of *a priori* truths; the resolution of a conflict of principles in a particular situation is held to be an intuition of preponderant 'weight' or 'stringency', comparable with a judgement about the relative weight of evidence for alternative solutions to an empirical problem. If it is unhelpful to speak of intuition, it is doubly so to use the same term for two different forms of judgement.

Utilitarianism says that the rational way of solving the priority problem is to regard the principle of utility as the court of appeal; where common rules of morality dictate conflicting courses of action in a particular situation, the right action is the one that seems likely to contribute most to the general happiness. This is the only rational method, according to utilitarianism, because the common rules of morality all depend on the more general principle of utility; for example, the rule of justice that merit should be rewarded holds good simply because actions called meritorious are actions that are generally useful and because the encouragement of such actions by the incentive of reward is useful.

The main difficulty with the utilitarian solution is that *some* moral principles, and especially some aspects of justice, do not seem to depend on utility. Where such a principle conflicts with another, an appeal to utility may seem irrelevant. Indeed, some of the most perplexing conflicts are conflicts between the principle of utility itself and an aspect of justice. This can be illustrated within the very theory of utilitarianism. The theory really consists of two principles, one prescribing the maximum increase of the total sum of happiness, the other prescribing the distribution of happiness to as many persons as possible. These two principles can conflict. In a particular situation an individual, or more realistically, a set of legislators, may be faced with two alternative policies. The first seems likely to increase the total national wealth more than the second, but the second seems likely to spread it more widely. Which policy is to be preferred? Utilitarianism gives us no answer.

Certain theories purport to do better than classical utilitarianism, at least verbally, by framing a single overriding principle. Thus, for example, one form of 'agathism' says that the single principle is to *realize* (not *produce*) a maximum of good; then equal or widespread distribution of happiness, no less than the production of means to happiness, can be called 'a realization of good'. In practice, of course, we are no better off, for we still have to decide how to measure the 'good' of wide distribution against the 'good' of increased total happiness. We start off with the problem of deciding which is 'right', and we end up simply by being told to switch our language from 'right' to 'better'. The problem itself remains.

Rawls makes the novel proposal that we should perhaps get away from looking for a single overriding principle and should instead rank moral principles in a 'lexical' or 'serial' order. By this he means giving priority to principle *A* until it is *fully* satisfied (or unless it does not apply) before we are allowed to move on to implement principle *B*, which in turn must be fully satisfied before we may move on to implement principle *C*, and so on. At his first introduction of the idea Rawls admits that it does not appear promising, and he expects to use it only in a limited way. Still, it is an interesting suggestion, and one looks forward to seeing it worked out later in the book.

In the end it is not worked out at any length. Rawls's proposal is that his first principle of justice (the claim of equal liberty) should be ranked first in the serial order, his second principle of justice (which stresses the claim of need) should be ranked second, and the principle of utility should be ranked third. If we are to take him seriously, this must mean (*a*) that in any conflict between equal liberty and need, the claim of liberty should prevail; (*b*) in any conflict between need and utility, the claim of need should prevail; and (*c*) in any conflict between liberty and utility, the claim of liberty should prevail. The first at least of these claims is confirmed by Rawls's own statement of his first priority rule: 'The principles of justice are to be ranked in lexical order and therefore liberty can be restricted only for the sake of liberty' (p. 302). This seems to imply that imprisonment is justified only for infringing or imperilling liberty, and not, e.g. for criminal negligence or for causing a nuisance.

How can the second principle of justice be implemented at all if the first principle has lexical priority? The first principle requires a maximum of equal liberty for all. The second says that inequalities (of liberty as of other things) are justified only if they benefit people in all positions and especially the least advantaged. Now if the first principle has lexical priority, this means that no question of inequality, even for the sake of benefiting the needy or the society as a whole, may be considered unless there is full satisfaction of the first principle, maximum equal liberty for all. A maximum of equal liberty is the same as a minimum of restraints on liberty equally for all. Restraints on a man's liberty, according to Rawls, are justified only as necessary means to the protection of a like liberty for others; so that all the restraints in a situation of maximum equal liberty are necessary for the protection of that maximum. Then if a restraint on liberty is lightened in one quarter, this must have the consequence of adding to the impediments to liberty in another quarter. In other words, any increase of liberty for one individual or group must involve a decrease of liberty for some other individual or group; it must involve a falling short of the maximum of equal liberty that existed before. So lexical priority for maximum equal liberty implies that unequal *liberty* may never be considered at all. And since many other inequalities (e.g. of wealth) involve unequal liberty, they may not be considered either.

Rawls states his priority rules about half-way through the book. He delays giving any argument for them until near the end, and when it does finally come it is restricted to presenting a case for the priority of liberty. The argument is that the value of liberty, as compared with other goods, rises as civilization progresses. '*Beyond some point* it becomes and then remains irrational from the standpoint of the original position to acknowledge a lesser liberty for the sake of greater material means and amenities of office' (p. 542, my italics). How does this help to show that liberty is to be given priority in a *lexical* series as explained earlier? That kind of priority means that the claims of liberty are to be satisfied as fully as possible *before* the claims of other goods are implemented at all. What Rawls is now saying is that, *after* certain other goods have been achieved up to some point, liberty comes to be preferred to a *further* increase in those other goods. This is brought out quite clearly on the next page. 'Until the basic wants of individuals can be fulfilled, the relative urgency of their interest in liberty cannot be firmly decided in advance. . . . But under favorable circumstances the fundamental interest in determining our plan of life eventually assumes a prior place' (p. 543). In other words, liberty is not prior to the satisfaction of 'basic wants'; liberty comes to the fore when and only when these basic wants are satisfied, and even then its priority over other goods is relative, not absolute. The original notion of lexical priority has disappeared completely.

Although the argument is unsatisfactory, at least there is an argument given in the end for assigning priority to Rawls's first principle of justice. When it comes to priority among goods, he is not so accommodating. He defines primary goods as 'things that every rational man is presumed to want' (p. 62), and he distinguishes natural primary goods, such as health and intelligence, from social primary goods. The social primary goods, he says, are liberty and opportunity, income and wealth, and self-respect. It seems odd to put income and wealth in the same category as liberty, opportunity, and self-respect. In the ordinary way one thinks of income and wealth as means to basic goods rather than as goods themselves; and since there are forms of society (some of them highly rational) in which income and wealth do not exist as private possessions, one expects some argument for classing them as 'things that every rational man is presumed to want'. The argument never comes. Rawls does explain why he thinks great importance is to be attached to liberty and to self-respect, but so far as the list of social goods as a whole is concerned he simply says that he will not argue the case for it 'since their claims seem evident enough' (p. 434).

Needless to say, there are many other features of this large and complex book that invite comment, but I have confined myself to two main theses because of their originality. Each of them, it seems to me, founders completely. Why then do I say that the book is an important one? Just because these two theses are novel and hold out the promise of new light on old problems.

8   Taking Law Seriously

The title of this essay indicates an intention to discuss Professor Ronald Dworkin's book, *Taking Rights Seriously* (1977). It also indicates some scepticism of the way in which he makes *rights* the central concept in his positive theory.

I hope that no apology is needed for a political theorist to take law seriously as part of his own professional concerns. Time was when students of Politics in British universities were expected, as a matter of course, to learn something about the law. But it was largely constitutional law, and that could be misleading because it tended to blind people to the difference between the formalities of law and the realities of political power. In political theory, however, it is beneficial to keep an eye on the law. You get one perspective on political concepts and principles if you think of them in the light of the actual working of political institutions; another if you think of them in relation to moral philosophy; and yet another if you relate them to jurisprudence. In many countries of the continent of Europe the philosophy of law has long been the basic discipline for the philosophy of action, and in the United States there has been a fruitful resurgence of legal and political philosophy in connection with each other. Here in Britain the work of Professor H. L. A. Hart has probably affected students of political theory more widely than it has affected students of law; and likewise his successor in the Oxford Chair of Jurisprudence, Ronald Dworkin, receives as much attention from political theorists as from teachers and students of jurisprudence. Dworkin himself is deeply interested in the interplay between law and politics, and indeed he takes up an active stance of political ideology more strongly than do many political theorists. I feel at times that his understanding of politics, at least in Britain, is not what it might be; but then I am quite sure that he could say the same of the understanding of law in the minds of most political theorists—I should certainly say this myself about my own very limited acquaintance with law. So perhaps each of us would do better to stick to his own last? Well, I do not think that political theory really has a last of its own. If it does not carry on its business in active partnership with political institutions, or moral philosophy, or law, it simply is nothing, or at any rate nothing serious—a rather pointless abstraction. And if people like myself deal with political theory *purely* in relation to moral philosophy, we are rightly accused of wearing blinkers. So it is best to widen our scope and try to see relationships. When we make mistakes, others will correct them.

i

Dworkin's book (like this one of mine) is a collection of essays mostly written for different occasions. In his Introduction he sees them all as contributing to a connected theory of law and gives a succinct statement of the purpose of the book: to criticize legal positivism and utilitarianism, and to replace them by 'the rights thesis'. The main part of this purpose is especially served by two of the essays, 'The Model of Rules I' and 'Hard Cases'. Of these, the former is the more clear and persuasive. It is the piece which made Dworkin known to scholars in Britain and it strikes me as the most effective paper in the collection.

Legal positivism is a theory of what law is, while utilitarianism, applied to law, is a theory of what it ought to be. Legal positivism, in contrast to natural law theory, maintains that law is logically independent of morals. Dworkin considers that the best modern version of legal positivism is the theory put forward by H. L. A. Hart in *The Concept of Law* (1961). He fastens upon Hart's account of law as a system of primary and secondary rules, and he criticizes it on the ground that a system of law includes 'principles' and 'policies' which must be distinguished from rules. These principles and policies are often moral in character, and therefore the thesis of legal positivism is disproved. As evidence for his view that a system of law goes beyond rules to principles and other standards, Dworkin cites certain cases, usually from American law but occasionally from English.

If, as he says, his purpose in this is to criticize legal positivism, then he has misplaced his target in concentrating on Hart's theory of primary and secondary rules. It is true that the concept of primary and secondary rules is the most distinctive, and the most original, feature in Hart's theory of law. It is also true that Hart, in his careful discussion of the controversy between natural law theory and legal positivism, comes down in the end on the side of legal positivism. But it is not true, as Dworkin appears to imply, that Hart regards Anglo-American law as consisting solely of rules unrelated to moral principle. At the end of his chapter on primary and secondary rules Hart says explicitly:

The union of primary and secondary rules is at the centre of a legal system; but it is not the whole, and as we move away from the centre we shall have to accommodate, in ways indicated in later chapters, elements of a different character.[1]

Those later chapters include discussion of the relation between law and morals. At one point Hart says this:

The law of every modern state shows at a thousand points the influence of both the accepted social morality and wider moral ideals. These influences enter into law either abruptly and avowedly through legislation, or silently and piecemeal through the judicial process. In some systems, *as in the United States*, the ultimate *criteria of legal validity* explicitly incorporate *principles* of justice or substantive moral values . . . [In this and in other systems] statutes may be a mere legal shell and demand by their express terms to be filled out with the aid of *moral principles* . . . No 'positivist' could deny that these are facts . . .[2]

Nevertheless, Hart sides with legal positivism because he recognizes that there have occasionally been legal systems, such as the law of Nazi Germany, which flouted traditional moral principles. While condemning such systems as much as anyone, Hart considers that we shall see more clearly the complex nature of the issues involved if we accept the proposition that law may be valid law although iniquitous. To this extent Hart supports legal positivism against natural law theory. But *that* defence of legal positivism is not weakened in the slightest by showing that the legal systems of the United States and England include a frequent reference to moral principle. Hart has acknowledged this in the clearest possible terms.

However, Hart does say that primary and secondary rules are at 'the centre' of a legal system and that they form its 'essence'.[3] Dworkin would no doubt wish to claim that this is not correct, that standards other than rules enter into the central character of law. Although his argument does nothing to disprove Hart's form of legal positivism, it may well require Hart's characterization of a legal system to be modified.

ii

The nub of the argument is given in 'The Model of Rules I', where Dworkin distinguishes 'rules' from other 'standards' (notably 'principles' and 'policies') which form part of a system of law. He says that when a court breaks new ground in a judgement, it often appeals to certain general principles which cannot be called rules and which are as much moral as legal. One of his examples is the case of *Riggs* v. *Palmer*, in which the law of inheritance was modified by invoking 'general, fundamental maxims of the common law' that no one should be allowed 'to profit by his own fraud, or to take advantage of his own wrong, or to found any claim upon his own iniquity, or to acquire property by his own crime'.[4] (Palmer, the man named as heir in the will, had murdered the testator in order to ensure that it would not be revoked.) Dworkin argues that such maxims or principles are different from legal rules because rules apply 'in an all-or-nothing fashion'[5] while principles incline without necessitating. Principles have a certain 'weight'[6] which must be taken into account but which does not of itself settle an issue. If in any particular case two or more principles conflict, a judgement must be formed about their relative weight or importance; one will be deemed paramount and so decisive, but this does not imply that the outweighed principle loses its force. By contrast, if two rules are found to conflict, one or other of them must be deemed to be invalid or must be revised (e.g. by specifying exceptions) so as to remove the conflict.

Critics have said that the facts adduced by Dworkin can be accommodated within the model of rules. What Dworkin calls a principle is embodied in the law as part of the judicial decision, and this certainly serves as a rule for the future. Nevertheless it seems to me that Dworkin's distinction retains its strength. What is the revised rule embodied in the decision of *Riggs*? Is it simply the narrow rule that a person named as heir in a properly executed will may not inherit if he has murdered the testator in order to do so? In that event, how do the wider formulations of principle in

the judgement enter into the matter? It seems proper to say that
Riggs laid down the narrow rule (that murder bars inheritance) *in
virtue of* the wider principle that a man should not be allowed by
law to benefit from his own wrong; but then the principle is the
ground of the rule and does not itself constitute the rule. Or would
the critics say that the revised rule embodied in *Riggs* is a wider
rule, corresponding to the so-called principle, that a person named
as heir in a properly executed will may not inherit if he thereby
would benefit by his own wrong? But that is doubtful, for Anglo-
American law does not always prevent a man from benefiting by
his own wrong. One can imagine a case where a person inheriting
under a will would thereby benefit from some relatively minor
wrong (e.g. he might have helped the testator to acquire his wealth
in business deals, one or two of which involved a breach of contract). Whatever the way in which the Anglo-American law of
inheritance may have developed since *Riggs*, the decision in *Riggs*
would not by itself clearly imply a decision adverse to my hypothetical heir. The principles or 'maxims' enunciated in the *Riggs*
judgement would have a certain force in the hypothetical case, but
there would also be a countervailing force in the precedents of
other leading cases which have allowed a man to gain some benefit
from relatively minor legal wrongs.

Riggs v. *Palmer* is an American case, and it may be thought that
courts in the United States are more liable than courts in England
to conform to Dworkin's pattern of allowing general moral principles to interfere with established legal practices. Although the
law of the United States is an offshoot of the English Common
Law, it exists in a different atmosphere because of the position of
the U.S. Supreme Court in interpreting the Constitution. Certainly the Supreme Court is less hidebound than the British House
of Lords in the latter's judicial capacity, precisely because the
Legislature in the U.S.A. does not possess the sovereignty—the
unlimited capacity to legislate—which is possessed by the U.K.
Parliament.

However, Dworkin's point can be illustrated from the practice
of English law as well as from American cases. The principle that
a person should not benefit from his own wrong is cited with some
frequency. In 1979 a young woman named Astrid Proll was
extradited to face serious criminal charges in West Germany. She

claimed that she should not be extradited because she had British nationality through her marriage, under an assumed name, to an Englishman. The case was heard by Sir George Baker, President of the Family Division of the High Court. He ruled that her marriage to the Englishman was valid but he nevertheless exercised judicial discretion in refusing to grant a declaration that she had acquired British nationality through the marriage. In the course of his judgement he said:[7]

Her entry and residence in this country had been achieved by lies, personation and fraud. . . . A person cannot achieve status by fraud. . . . No woman can take advantage of her own wrong. This court cannot and should not further the criminal acts of this woman and permit her to achieve an end by the course of conduct she had pursued.

Another instance is in the report of the Royal Commission on Standards of Conduct in Public Life (1976), headed by Lord Salmon, a Lord of Appeal in Ordinary. The report noted that the Inland Revenue allowed bribes, if described as 'commission', to be treated as tax-deductible expenses, and that they were not prepared to pass information to the Director of Public Prosecutions, even if they suspected that the company was engaged in corrupt practices. The Royal Commission attached no blame to the Inland Revenue, who were following an old practice.

The fact that the giving or receipt of the bribe happens to be a crime has been assumed to be irrelevant . . . This is because the well established and very salutary rule of law, that no man is entitled to take advantage of his own wrong, has been overlooked.[8]

I observe that the Royal Commission calls the principle a 'rule' of law and writes as if it should have been invoked; but one cannot infer from this that a court would require the Inland Revenue to disclose to the Director of Public Prosecutions information about bribes.

Here is a different example from English law, which raises the same kind of point as *Riggs* v. *Palmer*; that is to say, a principle is involved, but one which would not be applied universally. This particular principle is commonly described as a principle of 'natural justice' and is therefore especially apposite to the question whether law is logically independent of morals. The principle is that no man may be a judge in his own cause. It was applied in the case of *Dimes* v. *The Proprietors of the Grand Junction Canal*, 1852. A decision in favour of the company had been given by Lord Chancellor Cottenham, and this was set aside by the House of Lords on the ground that Lord Cottenham was a shareholder in the company. Professor Philip S. James comments:[9]

No doubt in fact his Lordship's decision was quite unbiased; but, as Lord Campbell said in his speech, it is essential that every tribunal should avoid even giving the appearance of having an interest in the subject-matter of an action before it. The courts will not, however, press the principle to extremes, and it will only operate where the situation is such that there is a real likelihood of bias in the member or members of the tribunal whose right to jurisdiction is impugned.

James seems to have slipped into inconsistency here. On the one hand he writes that Lord Cottenham's decision was 'no doubt . . . quite unbiased', and on the other hand he says that the principle will only operate where 'there is a real likelihood of bias'. However, I assume he has some authority for his view that the principle will not be applied by the courts in *all* cases, so that here, as with the principle in *Riggs*, it is inappropriate to think of it as a *rule*.

Yet another example may be cited from a case that went up to the House of Lords in 1978, *Hoskyn* v. *Metropolitan Police Commissioner*.[10] The question for decision was whether a wife was a compellable witness against her husband on a criminal charge. The case was one in which Mr. Hoskyn was accused of wounding a woman with intent to do grievous bodily harm. A few days before the initial trial came on, Mr. Hoskyn married the woman, and in consequence she was no longer keen to testify against him. Could she be compelled to do so? The trial judge and the Court of Appeal said yes, following an earlier ruling of 1931 by the Court of Criminal Appeal. The House of Lords said no and overruled the earlier case.

The ground for saying that a spouse was *not* a compellable witness was a long-standing principle of the Common Law, going back to Coke. It is that husband and wife have a unity of interest and that evidence by one against the other is liable to be a cause of 'implacable discord and dissention' between them. (The quoted phrase about discord comes from Coke himself, but not the words

I

'unity of interest', which were used by a later judge. Instead Coke referred, in Latin, to the biblical expression that husband and wife are 'one flesh', and as a result his argument was called by Bentham 'the grim-gibber,[11] nonsensical reason . . . of the identity of the two persons'.) In a case of 1912, *Leach* v. *R.*, Lord Chancellor Loreburn spoke of 'a fundamental and old principle' that a wife should not be compelled to give evidence against her husband on a criminal charge. Another of the judges in that case, Lord Atkinson, described it as a 'principle . . . deep seated in the common law of this country'. In Hoskyn's case Lord Wilberforce spoke of the 'general principles' applied in *Leach.*

The ground for saying that a spouse *should* be a compellable witness in a criminal case was given in a dissenting judgement by Lord Edmund-Davies. Quoting Lord Justice Geoffrey Lane in the Court of Appeal hearing, he argued that the general principle should not apply where a criminal charge was concerned: 'the interests of the state and members of the public' required that evidence of a crime should be freely available to the court trying the crime.

Lord Edmund-Davies prefaced his judgement with a statement making two general points about adjudication, both of them interestingly explicit in the mouth of a judge when adjudicating: that judges at times are obliged to *make* law, and that on such occasions their criterion should be public utility:

. . . when your Lordships' House is called upon to determine a question of law regarding which there are no binding precedents and no authorities directly in point, and where it has accordingly to perform an act of law-making, I apprehend that the decision will largely turn upon what is thought most likely to advance the public weal.[12]

In the opposing judgements of Lord Wilberforce and Lord Edmund-Davies there is a conflict between a principle and a policy (to use Dworkin's terminology). Can we put it in terms of rules? We can say that the rule that a competent witness is compellable is subject to exception in the case of witness by one spouse against another. But what counts as a *principle* in the Common Law is not the consequent rule that a spouse should not be compelled. The principle is the *ground* of the consequent rule, namely the fact that husband and wife have a single interest and that compellability as a witness is liable to cause dissension. Similarly, what counts as a *principle* or *policy* on the other side is not the rule that competent witnesses are generally compellable, but the ground or reason for insisting on this in a criminal case, namely the interest of the State or the public in having a crime cleared up. The two *ethical* considerations (family unity and public interest) have to be balanced against each other. When the House of Lords decided, by a majority of four to one, that the principle of Common Law should be decisive, this did not mean that Lord Edmund-Davies's policy was deemed to have no validity.

I conclude that Dworkin's criticism of the model of rules is amply justified. Analytical philosophy in recent decades has shown an excessive fondness for the word 'rules'. So-called 'rules of language' and 'moral rules' have often been compared with the rules of a game. The analogy has point at times, but it can also seriously mislead. The norms on which moral judgement is based often need to be *contrasted* with the rules of a game or the rules of etiquette. Dworkin is quite right to say, in 'The Model of Rules II' when replying to a criticism, that so-called moral rules are not rules at all and that the language of principle is more apt than that of rule to describe standards in morals.[13]

iii

In 'The Model of Rules I' Dworkin concentrates on the distinction between rules and other standards used in law. In 'Hard Cases' he turns his attention to the distinction, within those other standards, between principle and policy, relying upon this to develop his second main purpose, a criticism of utilitarianism as an account of what law ought to be. He takes the utilitarian view to be that social utility is the only proper criterion for making new laws. He regards policies as standards that are aggregative and have regard to a collective goal, while principles are distributive and have regard to the rights of individuals. It is not easy to follow the main thread of the argument in this paper, since it becomes entangled in a rather confusing set of dichotomies of rights—absolute and non-absolute, background and institutional, abstract and concrete. However, it seems that Dworkin would be ready to accept the utilitarian thesis for legislation but not for adjudication, and a secondary theme of this essay is the supposition that his opponents treat adjudication as an imitation of, and substitute for, legislation. His own view is that while policy occasionally enters into the adjudication of hard cases, the new law that comes into being from the adjudication of hard cases is characteristically generated by a regard for principle. So far as I can see, the core of his argument against the utilitarian thesis is that the use of precedent in adjudication implies emphasis on the principle of fairness that like cases should be treated alike. A legislature, so he says, does not have to worry about this principle, e.g. in awarding subsidies to manufacturers from one month to another; it need have regard only for public utility, and is under no obligation to treat one manufacturer this month in the same way that it treated another last month.

Some features of this argument seem to me unsatisfactory. First, the essay gives the impression (no doubt unintentionally) that adjudication generates new law only in hard cases. Are hard cases any different from others for the purposes of Dworkin's argument? Adjudication in civil law cases (in courts above the first tier) almost always generates new law to some modest degree. If the law as applied to a particular dispute is clear, the case is normally settled out of court. Adjudication is called for only because there is some doubt or obscurity in the scope of precedent or statute as applying to the case in question. Once this is recognized, the idea that adjudication is a substitute for legislation loses all plausibility.[14]

Secondly, it seems odd (at least to those more familiar with the British than the American system of government) to cite the award of subsidies to manufacturers as a characteristic activity of a *legislature*. In legislation proper, while public utility is and should be the first consideration, principles of fairness, and of establishing and protecting rights for individuals and groups, play quite a large role too. Parliamentary debate on Bills, and civil service discussion on proposals for legislation, are rarely confined to differences of opinion about ends and means; questions of fairness keep coming up all the time.

Let me give some examples from actual and potential legislation in recent years. The Industrial Relations Act 1971, and its successor, the Employment Protection Act 1975, contain provisions about 'unfair dismissal' which are as important and substantial as anything in those two Acts. There is no suggestion that these provisions are designed to secure general utility; on the contrary, many people would and do argue that these provisions militate against the *general* well-being. Their purpose is avowedly to secure *fairness* for individuals. The Sex Discrimination Act and the Race Relations Acts are likewise clearly aimed at fairness, not utility. The Equal Opportunities Commission, in stimulating public discussion on possible changes in the tax laws, again has in mind the elimination of unfairness. Proposed clauses for voting by Proportional Representation, which were debated in Parliament at the committee stage of the Bills for devolution in Scotland and Wales, were concerned with fairness rather than utility.

Thirdly, while it is true that, in adjudication, considerations of justice play a far larger part than those of public policy, a utilitarian need not be greatly worried by what Dworkin says about the use of precedent. Consistency as between one case and another is as useful as it is fair (because it makes for 'certainty'), and corresponds to the universality of a statute.

In fact, even if we are not utilitarians, we should, I think, regard adherence to precedent as resting upon utility rather than justice.[15] P. S. James, in his textbook cited earlier, writes that the practical reason for conforming to precedent is the desirability 'that decisions shall be uniform, for it is often asserted that it is more important that the law shall be certain than that it shall always promote justice in individual cases'.[16] This implies that the certainty afforded by conformity to precedent is commonly held to be independent of issues of justice. So does the considered judgement of Lord Diplock in the case of *Davis* v. *Johnson*,[17] supporting the doctrine of precedent by the need for certainty and contrasting that with 'the proper development of the law'. He clearly regarded the ground of the rule of *stare decisis* as lying in the importance of certainty and *not* in being *fair* as between one case and another.

It would be a moral mistake to say that a court which thought a previous decision wrong should follow it in the interests of fairness. You cannot justify a decision as fair, *simply* on the ground that it is in line with earlier decisions. You must have reason to regard the earlier decisions as inherently just or reasonable. If, in the past, outspoken critics have been silenced, that does not make it fair to silence outspoken critics today; or if, in the past, those ill-endowed by nature have been allowed to starve, that does not make it fair to let the ill-endowed starve today. It is fair to treat like cases alike, *provided* that you do not thereby maintain an inherent injustice.

iv

The third element of Dworkin's purpose in his book is to replace legal positivism and utilitarianism by 'the rights thesis'. Having argued that the making of law, at least in adjudication, does and should include general moral principles (other than the principle of utility), he now wants to show that these principles are essentially propositions about rights—rights as contrasted with goals, but also as contrasted with duties. It is perhaps natural to think of rights as more basic than duties in an analysis of law, but in the present context Dworkin is avowedly talking of principles and rights that are in the first instance moral rather than legal. (Not infrequently he talks also of political rights, but I take it that he regards these as a species of moral rights.) I cannot see why he should think that moral principles are more accurately described as rights-principles than as duties-principles or as duties-cum-rights-principles. In the essay on 'Justice and Rights' he says that duty-based political theories treat codes of conduct 'as of the essence', while right-based theories treat codes of conduct 'as instrumental, perhaps necessary to protect the rights of others, but having no essential value in themselves'.[18] The only example cited in the paragraph is Kant as a duty-based theorist; but in a later essay Dworkin says that the first essential for taking *rights* seriously is the idea of human dignity and he cites Kant as the best-known advocate of that notion.[19]

It seems to me that Dworkin has not made out an adequate case for giving a primacy to moral rights as contrasted with duties or obligations. He says in 'Hard Cases' that if one man is drowning and another can save him with little risk to himself, then the first man has a moral right to be saved by the second. Some people would question whether it is proper to talk of the first man as having a right, but would certainly agree that the second man has an obligation. In 'The Model of Rules I' Dworkin makes much of the principle, used in the *Riggs* judgement, that a man should not be allowed to benefit from his own wrong. Is this a rights principle?

It can of course be stated in the form, 'A man who has committed a wrong has no right to benefit thereby', but this negative statement surely does not have the force required for the purpose. The point of the principle is far better expressed by saying that the courts, acting as the guardian of the community, have a duty, so far as they have the power, to prevent the wrongdoer from benefiting by his wrong.[20] Again, in developing his rights thesis in later essays, Dworkin maintains that the fundamental right is a right to equal concern and respect. The final words of this formula show that the principle advocated would be stated more clearly in terms of duty or obligation. An agent can show concern and respect for others and can try to do so to an equal degree for everyone with whom he comes into contact. I can make sense of an alleged right to equal concern and respect only by interpreting it as a roundabout way of describing an obligation to others which Dworkin would like to impose on us all.

This leads me to Dworkin's characterization of his view as 'a liberal theory of law'.[21] He presumably uses the word 'liberal' in its American rather than its British sense. It is certainly a surprise to find a professed liberal arguing that there is no right to liberty as such (but then it turns out that he means 'right' in the sense of an entrenched constitutional right) and that the basic right is to a form of equality rather than liberty. It is again a surprise to find him arguing in favour of reverse discrimination, on the ground that the *social goal* served by this policy outweighs the sense of injustice felt by the *individual* who is discriminated against.[22] After this it is less of a surprise to be told, in an essay entitled 'Liberty and Liberalism', that J.S. Mill 'was a socialist'.[23] Of course there is some evidence which can be said to support that proposition (and a great deal more which counts against it), but Dworkin does not bother to say what it is. In this essay he mercilessly belabours Gertrude Himmelfarb for her interpretation of Mill's essay *On Liberty*. Her book[24] does indeed call for criticism, but I doubt if she is much worried by Dworkin's charge that her 'huge misunderstanding' arises from confusing liberty as license with liberty as independence.[25] In the final paragraph of the essay we learn that she is not alone, since the same confusion has been made by the United States Supreme Court, by conservatives generally, and by radicals generally. Miss Himmelfarb might well feel that in these circumstances she prefers to be 'out of step' together with this goodly company.

Dworkin's defence of the rights thesis, as he understands it, could do with elaboration. He wants to make equality rather than liberty the central concept. The basic right to equality is not equality of treatment or even of opportunity, but equality of concern and respect. These are vague terms. Dworkin purports to explain them on p. 272. To treat people with concern, he says, is to treat them 'as human beings who are capable of suffering and frustration', and to treat them with respect is to treat them 'as human beings who are capable of forming and acting on intelligent conceptions of how their lives should be lived'. As it stands, this will not do. A torturer treats his victims as capable of suffering and frustration and as capable of forming and acting on intelligent conceptions, etc. His torture would have no point if he did not treat them as such.

Dworkin goes on to say that a government must treat people with *equal* concern and respect, but he does not explain why. If respect is due to human beings because they are capable of forming and acting on intelligent conceptions of how their lives should be lived, and if (as is surely the case) human beings have that capability in different degrees, why should not the respect due to them vary in accordance with their degree of capability? The case for some form of equalitarianism needs to be made with great care, certainly greater than is shown in this book.

My conclusions may be summarized as follows. Dworkin makes out his case for the first of his three theses: law does not consist of rules alone; it includes principles and other 'standards' which are not exclusive to it but are shared with the domain of morality. He does not make out his case for his second and third theses. As regards utilitarianism, Dworkin is mistaken in arguing that legislation is guided only by utility. He is also mistaken in what seems to be his main (or at least *a* main) argument for the view that adjudication emphasizes fairness rather than utility; I agree with the view but not with the argument for it, drawn from the use of precedent. On the rights thesis, again I am prepared to agree with Dworkin's view that *legal* rights are more basic than legal duties, but his account of the rights thesis applies it to rights which are moral as much as legal; and I cannot see that he has produced any sound argument or evidence for the opinion that *moral* rights are more basic than moral duties. Within the sphere of moral rights, I do not agree that some sort of basic right to equality is more fundamental than some sort of basic right to liberty, and Dworkin's arguments for this view carry no conviction whatever as they now stand.

9 Reverse Discrimination

i

It is somewhat ironic that a hard-boiled version of legal positivism (or 'realism') should have flourished in the United States, where decisions of the Supreme Court often have a 'natural law flavour'[1] and offer the clearest example of the role of moral principle in the administration of law. In our own generation at least, the Supreme Court may justly be called the conscience of the nation. A recent illustration is provided by the Bakke case.[2] The decision in that case is nothing like so momentous as many in the history of the Supreme Court, but it is likely to be a landmark in its practical effects. For legal and social philosophy it is instructive as an excellent example of the dilemmas of social justice. The debate in the recorded opinions of the judges, and the narrow majorities in their divided conclusions, reflect the finely balanced differences of judgement among thoughtful Americans on a conflict of moral principles.

Something of the same sort can occasionally be found in judgements of the highest courts in Britain, but to a much more limited degree. Although not a lawyer, I have read a certain number of English law reports for their bearing on issues of political theory and legal philosophy. Coming for the first time to read a full report of a judgement of the U.S. Supreme Court, I was struck by several differences. There is an atmosphere both of greater freedom and of greater authority. The latter is natural enough, for the Supreme Court does have an authority in relation to Acts of the U.S. Congress which no British court can have in relation to Acts of the sovereign U.K. Parliament. No doubt this is a major factor in inducing the Supreme Court to take a wide view of its responsibilities, to act as the mouthpiece of Natural Justice far more readily than any British court, to be at once practical and philosophical. But there is more to it than that. The greater freedom of the Supreme Court seems to me to be typical of a general difference between American and British institutions. We are more traditional, more conservative, more cautious. (This attitude is not at all irrational; I am speaking of social institutions, not of conduct in private life.) Americans are more ready to innovate, more bold, even, one may say, more rash. At any rate the Supreme Court, while always careful to avoid breaches of precedent, is clearly conscious that it is expected to give a lead, to follow its vision of justice for the present and the future rather than to be bound by a past outlook which may now be defective. The judges continually invoke precedent by quoting from earlier judgements of the court, but they are also prepared to give weight to the opinions of academic lawyers and of other thoughtful persons who have presented written submissions as *amici curiae*.

I noted, too, that the Supreme Court has recently decided that its interpretation of Acts of Congress may be aided by reference to the debates in both Houses when the relevant Bills were debated.[3] Judges on both sides of the fence in the Bakke case quoted statements by Representatives and Senators in promoting the passage through Congress of the Civil Rights Act of 1964. This current practice of the Supreme Court may be contrasted with the fate of a recent attempt by Lord Denning to refer to Hansard in order to elucidate the meaning of a phrase in a statute; he was promptly slapped down by the House of Lords.[4] If the Bakke case is any guide, however, the newly acquired practice of the Supreme Court does not seem to confer an advantage. The interpretation of statute came up because one leg of Bakke's case was that the University of California had contravened a statutory prohibition of discrimination on the ground of race, colour, or national origin. The university submitted that the clause in the statute was intended to protect ethnic minorities and to prohibit discrimination against them, not to prohibit also reverse discrimination in their favour. As you might expect, reference to debates on the Bill in the two Houses of Congress enabled the judges to produce quotations which could be taken to support either view, (a) that the purpose of the clause was to protect ethnic minorities from being discriminated against, and (b) that nevertheless it would also have the effect of prohibiting discrimination against anyone on the ground of race, colour, or national origin. The result in fact was precisely the one envisaged in the traditional argument used in Britain (and recently restated by the House of Lords in *Davis* v. *Johnson*), namely that going beyond the plain meaning of the words of a statute is liable to increase, not to decrease, uncertainty.

Another interesting feature of the Supreme Court proceedings is that the report of the opinions delivered by the judges contains their added notes, some strengthening a point with detailed evidence, others criticizing an argument or assumption employed on the other side by fellow-judges or *amici curiae*. This, of course, enhances the value of the report for scholars, and especially for those concerned with the philosophy of law.

ii

The basic facts of the Bakke case are well known. Allan Bakke applied for admission to the Medical School of the University of California at Davis. He was not admitted despite having a rating, in terms of academic record and other relevant qualities, higher than that of candidates who were admitted under a special programme for ethnic minorities. Bakke took the university to court on the ground that it had discriminated against him illegally. When the case was finally disposed of by the U.S. Supreme Court, the judges, by a majority of one, upheld Bakke's claims, but this simple conclusion was complicated by the fact that one member of the majority also agreed with the minority that discrimination in favour of blacks and other ethnic minorities could be justifiable. Thus there was a majority of one against the kind of reverse discrimination practised at Davis, and a majority of one in favour of other possible forms of reverse discrimination.

The Supreme Court's judgement was widely discussed in the daily and weekly newspapers. I did not have the opportunity to read at first hand the comments of any American journalists, but I did read quite a number of discussions in the British press (and heard a sound radio 'Letter from America' on the subject by Alistair Cooke). Since these frequently quoted or referred to what was said in American newspapers, they were probably typical of American comment also. The general impression conveyed by the journalists was that the mixed judgement of the court represented a compromise, in one way welcome, in another not.

(1) The welcome feature was that the judgement gave some

satisfaction to two opposed groups of enlightened Americans. One group had feared that reverse discrimination in favour of blacks would erode traditional liberal rights. The decision in favour of Bakke reassured them. The other group feared that a judgement for Bakke would halt, indeed turn back, the movement for 'affirmative action' to improve the position of blacks in the United States. While they were disappointed with the decision on Bakke and the University of California, they were comforted by the majority opinion in favour of other forms of affirmative action.

(2) The unwelcome feature was the (allegedly) confusing character of the outcome. The distinction, drawn by a single but decisive opinion, between the illegality of a quota system and the legality of a non-quota system of reverse discrimination, was specious (so the journalists said), since it made no real difference to the practical results. If the results were the same in practice, how could one say that an *overt* quota was all that mattered? And how could a university know whether its discriminatory programme would be held to involve a quota or not? The judgement of the court left the problem unresolved, the dilemma unaffected.

This summary of the bare bones of the case is true enough, so far as it goes, and the reaction of the journalists is fair enough. But they conceal some important features of the judges' arguments, and a reading of the complete report of the Supreme Court's decision shows that the abbreviated story given above is too crude.

Let me first fill out some factual detail. Allan Bakke applied for admission to the Davis Medical School on two occasions, first in 1973, at a late date, and then in 1974, in good time. The Medical School admitted 100 students each year. It had two programmes for admission, a general one and a special one. Of the 100 places, 16 were reserved for applicants under the special programme. This programme was advertised as available to candidates from 'economically and/or educationally disadvantaged backgrounds', and the information distributed to candidates said that 'ethnic minorities are not categorically considered under the Task Force [i.e. the special] program unless they are from disadvantaged backgrounds'. Each year the special programme attracted a large number of applicants from ethnic minorities and also a fair number of whites. Both these categories of applicants under the special programme claimed that they had a disadvantaged background. In 1973, there were 297 applicants under the special programme, 224 of them belonging to ethnic minorities and 73 being white. In 1974, there were 628 applicants, 456 belonging to ethnic minorities and 172 being white. In practice no whites were admitted under the special programme, not only in these two years but also in the preceding years in which the special programme was operated. The California Supreme Court concluded, and the university did not deny, 'that white applicants could not compete for the 16 places reserved solely for the special admissions program'.[5] This despite the continued advertisement of the special programme as available for any student from a disadvantaged background. In the report of the U.S. Supreme Court, Mr. Justice Powell observed: 'Despite the program's purported emphasis on disadvantage, it was a minority enrollment program with a secondary disadvantage element. White disadvantaged students were never considered under the special program, and the University acknowledges that its goal in devising the program was to increase minority enrollment.'[6]

In aiming at that goal the special programme had a reasonable measure of success. Over a period of four years 63 students from ethnic minorities were admitted under the special programme, as compared with 44 students from ethnic minorities accepted under the general programme with its higher academic requirements. I say that it had only a 'reasonable' measure of success because there is one odd feature in the statistics. The students admitted under the special programme belonged to three ethnic groups, blacks, Chicanos (Mexican–Americans), and Asians. Mr. Justice Powell noted that the university could not explain why only these three groups of ethnic minorities were favoured, and commented that the inclusion of Asians was 'especially curious in light of the substantial numbers of Asians admitted through the regular admissions process'.[7] In 1973, 2 Asians were admitted under the special programme and 13 under the general; in 1974, the figures were 4 special and 5 general; over the period 1970–4, 12 Asians were admitted under the special programme and 41 under the general.

The difference between the two programmes was this. Applicants under the general programme had to get over an initial hurdle of a fairly high average of academic grades before they could be considered for interview; applicants under the special programme did not. Those applicants under the special programme who were selected for interview competed only against each other for the reserved 16 places; they were not compared with any applicants under the general programme. The result, of course, was that a number of applicants under the general programme, including Bakke, were not admitted although their rating was higher than that of applicants admitted under the special programme. The final ratings on which admission depended were the result of interviews by five or six interviewers, each of whom was expected to take account, not only of academic record, but also of letters of recommendation, extra-curricular activities, and biographical data. Under the special programme the biographical information considered will no doubt have included the claim to be economically and/or educationally disadvantaged.

In 1973, applicants were seen by five interviewers, each of whom assigned a mark out of a maximum of 100 points. In 1974, there were six interviewers. Bakke's first application in 1973 was late, at a time when applicants under the general programme were being rejected if their total score was less than 470 out of 500. Bakke obtained a score of 468 and so was rejected. He sent in an appeal, which was considered, and turned down, by a particular member of staff of the university. In the following year, Bakke applied in good time. On this occasion he obtained a total score of 549 out of 600 and he was again rejected. It will be observed that his total score was better in 1973 (93.6%) than in 1974 (91.5%). The drop in his total for 1974 seems to have been to an unfortunate circumstance which does not help the appearance of the university's case. The member of staff who considered Bakke's appeal in 1973 happened to be the person assigned to report on his personality in 1974. This man gave Bakke a relatively low mark, with adverse comment, although the parallel report by another person in 1973 had stated that in personality Bakke was admirably suited for the medical profession. However, this does not affect the main issue. It was agreed that Bakke's total score would have secured him admission if there had not been a special programme reserving 16 places for applicants from ethnic minorities, many or all of whom obtained a lower total score than Bakke did.

Bakke based his case on the ground that the special programme operated so as to exclude him on the basis of race, in violation of his rights under: (a) the Equal Protection Clause of the Fourteenth

Amendment to the U.S. Constitution, which prohibits a State from denying 'to any person within its jurisdiction the equal protection of the laws'; (b) Article I, § 21, of the California Constitution, which provides that no citizen shall be granted privileges or immunities which are not granted upon the same terms to all citizens; and (c) § 601 of Title VI of the Civil Rights Act of 1964, which states that 'No person in the United States shall, on the ground of race, color, or national origin, be excluded from participation in, be denied the benefits of, or be subjected to discrimination under any program or activity receiving Federal financial assistance'.

The court of first instance which heard the case held that the university's special admissions programme was illegal. The court refused, however, to order the university to admit Bakke to the Medical School, because it held that the evidence which had been presented to it did not clearly demonstrate that Bakke would have been accepted were it not for the special programme. The university appealed to the Supreme Court of California against the ruling that its special programme was illegal. At the same time the university stated explicitly that, if it had not operated the special programme, Bakke would have been admitted under the general programme. The Supreme Court of California affirmed the view of the lower court that the special admissions programme was illegal. In the light of this ruling and of the statement by the university about the particular position of Bakke, the court added an order that Bakke be now admitted. Thereupon the university appealed to the U.S. Supreme Court.

The opinions of the judges of the U.S. Supreme Court were delivered after a lengthy interval, during which, no doubt, they considered and reconsidered views initially expressed by their members in the light of the arguments presented at the hearing and in depositions made by numerous *amici curiae*. Three main opinions were delivered. (Two of the four judges who found in favour of the university added short judgements on particular aspects but these do not alter the main substance of their position.)

(1) Four judges (Stevens J., Burger C. J., Stewart J., and Rehnquist J.) affirmed the judgement of the California Supreme Court, (a) holding that the special admissions programme was illegal, and (b) ordering that Bakke be admitted.

(2) Four judges (Brennan J., White J., Marshall J., and Blackmun J.) held that race may be considered in university admissions programmes, and therefore that the Davis Medical School was not acting illegally in operating its special programme and thereby rejecting Bakke.

(3) One judge (Powell J.) agreed with the first group of judges in holding that the special programme at Davis was illegal and that Bakke must therefore be admitted. But he also agreed with the second group of judges in holding that race may be considered in university admissions programmes.

Because the first two opinions were each held by four judges, the opinion of Mr. Justice Powell was treated as the judgement of the court. While he agreed with Justices Brennan, White, Marshall, and Blackmun that race may be considered in admissions programmes, he drew a distinction between programmes with a quota, which prevented some candidates from being considered on their individual merits, and other programmes, which took account of race as one relevant factor but considered each candidate individually in the light of all relevant factors (including race).

iii

The opinions of the judges produced decisions on three issues: (1) whether the special programme at Davis was legal; (2) more generally, whether it was legal to take account of race in admissions programmes; (3) whether the Medical School at Davis should be required to admit Bakke. On issues (1) and (3) it is quite clear that five judges took one view and four judges the contrary view. Five judges held that the special programme at Davis was illegal and that the university should be ordered to admit Bakke; four judges held that the special programme was legal and that therefore the university should not be required to admit Bakke.

On the more general issue (2), whether it was legal to take account of race in admissions programmes, the position is not so clear cut. The discussions by journalists of the court's ruling often gave the impression that on this matter, too, there were five judges in favour of the proposition (not the same five as were joined on the other two issues), and four judges against the proposition. This is not correct. There were certainly five judges in favour of the

K

proposition, and accordingly the proposition is now a part of U.S. law. But the other four judges did not say that they thought it illegal to take account of race in admissions programmes. What they said was that this question did not arise and that therefore, in their opinion, the court should not pronounce upon it *in this case.*

They had two connected reasons for that view. First, the U.S. Supreme Court was dealing with an appeal from the judgement of the California Supreme Court. The California Supreme Court had ruled on the two specific issues, whether the Davis special programme was illegal, and whether Davis should be ordered to admit Bakke. The task of the U.S. Supreme Court was to consider the appeal against the ruling of the court below. Having found that the ruling of the court below was correct in both its parts, the U.S. Supreme Court had fulfilled its task. It was improper for the court, in dealing with this case, to go on to any further issue.

Secondly, Mr. Justice Stevens, speaking on behalf of the four judges concerned, observed that it was the 'settled practice' of the U.S. Supreme Court 'to avoid the decision of a constitutional issue if a case can be fairly decided on a statutory ground'.[8] Bakke had based his claim against the university on three grounds, a clause in the U.S. Constitution, a provision in the California Constitution, and a provision of a statute, the Civil Rights Act of 1964. The claim was challenged by the university on all three grounds. According to Mr. Justice Stevens and his colleagues, 'only if petitioner [the university] should prevail on the statutory issue would it be necessary to decide whether the University's admissions program violated the Equal Protection Clause of the Fourteenth Amendment'.[9] The four judges considered that the special admissions programme violated the provision of the Civil Rights Act and that the case could and should be disposed of simply by reference to that statute.

Mr. Justice Stevens concluded: 'Accordingly, I concur in the Court's judgment insofar as it affirms the judgment of the Supreme Court of California. To the extent that it purports to do anything else, I respectfully dissent.'[10] The dissent is not from the proposition that it is legal to take account of race in admissions programmes. It is from the proposition that the court was called upon to consider the issue at all. Earlier in his judgement Mr. Justice Stevens said this:

This is not a class action. The controversy is between two specific litigants. . . . If the state court was correct in its view that the University's special program was illegal, and that Bakke was therefore unlawfully excluded from the medical school because of his race, we should affirm its judgment, *regardless of our views about the legality of admissions programs that are not now before the Court.*[11]

In the discussions of the journalists, it was suggested that if the view of Mr. Justice Stevens and his colleagues had prevailed, this would have put a stop to the whole movement of 'affirmative action' to give increased opportunities of higher education to blacks and other ethnic minorities. The assumption was that these four judges had pronounced positively against all forms of reverse discrimination. This assumption was mistaken. The four judges had refused to pronounce either way. If their view had prevailed, it would have been necessary to bring another case before the Supreme Court in order to obtain a ruling on the question whether any consideration of race in admissions programmes could be legal.

I suspect that this is why Mr. Justice Powell, at least, was ready to conduct his argument largely in terms of the Equal Protection Clause of the Fourteenth Amendment to the U.S. Constitution, and to produce a definitive ruling which allowed admissions programmes to discriminate in favour of ethnic minorities so long as they gave positive consideration to all individuals. The Bakke case was not the first occasion on which the U.S. Supreme Court was asked to pronounce on the legality of reverse discrimination in a university admissions programme. The same issue had come up a few years earlier in the case of a student named DeFunis,[12] whose application for admission to a Law School had been rejected although applicants with lower ratings, but from ethnic minorities, had been admitted under a procedure rather similar to the special admissions programme of the Davis Medical School. In the DeFunis case, the Supreme Court did not reach a decision. Because a lower court had found in favour of DeFunis, the Law School had admitted him and had said that it would allow him to complete the course irrespective of the outcome of its appeal to the Supreme Court. In consequence the court held that there was nothing for it to decide—on the particular case—and dismissed the appeal. This attitude was, of course, in line with that of Mr. Justice

Stevens and his colleagues in the Bakke case: a court should confine itself to the particular case before it and should not decide more than it has to. However, one of the members of the Supreme Court which heard the DeFunis case, Mr. Justice Douglas, thought that the court should not be so cautious. He wrote a dissenting opinion to the effect that the claim of DeFunis, that he had been illegally discriminated against, was valid in terms of the Equal Protection Clause of the Fourteenth Amendment. The judge also went on to suggest that universities could achieve their aim of favouring ethnic minorities by using a different sort of procedure which would not violate the Equal Protection Clause. In short, Mr. Justice Douglas (who had retired by the time *Bakke* came up) foreshadowed the view held by Mr. Justice Powell in *Bakke*. Although Mr. Justice Douglas's opinion in *DeFunis* was not decisive, being a single minority view, it was taken by many educational institutions to be 'handwriting on the wall',[13] likely to be confirmed by the Supreme Court when a substantially similar case to *DeFunis* came before it. *Bakke* was precisely that substantially similar case. All Americans who were at all concerned about the problems of conscience raised by the history of blacks in the United States, were waiting to see whether the Supreme Court would indeed confirm the opinion of Mr. Justice Douglas in *DeFunis* or would allow quota admissions programmes to be legal. They would have felt thoroughly frustrated if the Supreme Court had once again ducked the issue of general principle on the ground that the particular appeal before it did not require a decision on the wider question.

It appears to me that, from a strictly legal point of view, at any rate in the tradition of Anglo–American law, Mr. Justice Stevens and his colleagues were correct to hold (*a*) that the court should not go beyond the particular issues of the appeal before it, unless it had to, and (*b*) that since the settled practice of the court is to avoid a constitutional issue when a case can be fairly decided on a statutory ground, then the court should stick to that settled practice, if it can. But with *Bakke* coming hard on the heels of *DeFunis*, and with the dissenting opinion of Mr. Justice Douglas in *DeFunis* hanging suspended in mid-air (or on Professor Dworkin's wall), it was not possible, or at least not sensible, politically speaking, for the court to confine itself to a narrowly legal view of its duty.

However, it is important to observe that the majority of five to four, allowing reverse discrimination of a kind, was not a bare majority of one in favour of that *policy*. It was a bare majority of one in favour of *declaring* a policy. We have no reason to suppose that the four judges in the minority would necessarily have dissented from the policy itself if they had thought it proper to express an opinion on that matter. Nor have we any reason to suppose that they would have favoured the policy. The vote was five in favour and four abstaining, not five in favour and four against.

It is also worth repeating that Mr. Justice Powell's decisive opinion in *Bakke* was, in principle, a reaffirmation of Mr. Justice Douglas's minority opinion in *DeFunis*. Some of the popular discussion of the court's ruling in the Bakke case suggested that the distinction between an illegal quota system and a legal non-quota system was an unfortunate invention of Mr. Justice Powell. It may or may not be unfortunate, but it was not his invention. Critics should have foreseen that the similar distinction drawn earlier by Mr. Justice Douglas was likely to be endorsed in the Bakke case by some member or members of the Supreme Court.

iv

Let us now consider whether the distinction itself was unfortunate. Mr. Justice Powell did not attach any special significance to the idea of a quota as such. At an early point in his judgement he wrote:

... the parties fight a sharp preliminary action over the proper characterization of the special admissions program. Petitioner [the university] prefers to view it as establishing a 'goal' of minority representation in the medical school. Respondent [Bakke], echoing the courts below, labels it a racial quota.

This semantic distinction is beside the point: the special admissions program is undeniably a classification based on race and ethnic background.[14]

Now the alternative methods of giving preference to racial minorities, which Mr. Justice Powell, and his predecessor Mr. Justice Douglas, would allow, were certainly methods of reaching a 'goal' of minority representation. So if Mr. Justice Powell regards talk of a 'quota' as merely a 'semantic distinction' and 'beside the point', what exactly is his objection to the kind of programme followed at Davis? It is that this programme did not give consideration to each applicant as an *individual*. Mr. Justice Powell argues, quoting earlier judgements of the Supreme Court, that the reference to 'persons', in the Equal Protection Clause of the Fourteenth Amendment, means that the rights guaranteed by the clause are 'guaranteed to the individual'. 'The guarantee of equal protection cannot mean one thing when applied to one individual and something else when applied to a person of another color.'[15] Mr. Justice Powell thinks that the Davis programme infringes this constitutional requirement, but that the kind of programme used at Harvard and Princeton does not. The latter method allows some weight to be given to an applicant's ethnic background as one factor among others, just as weight might be given to an applicant's rural background or some other relevant matter. The ethnic factor can tip the balance and enable one applicant to be preferred over another because the first comes from a disadvantaged ethnic group, but both applicants have been considered individually. The second applicant *might* have had some other factor in his favour which could have outweighed the preference given to disadvantaged ethnic minorities.

'This kind of program treats each applicant as an individual in the admissions process. The applicant who loses out on the last available seat to another candidate receiving a "plus" on the basis of ethnic background will not have been foreclosed from all consideration for that seat simply because he was not the right color or had the wrong surname. It would mean only that his combined qualifications, which may have included similar nonobjective [meaning 'non-academic', or perhaps 'non-quantifiable'?] factors, did not outweigh those of the other applicant. His qualifications would have been weighed fairly and competitively, and he would have no basis to complain of unequal treatment under the Fourteenth Amendment.'[16] In a note to this statement, Mr. Justice Powell added: 'The denial to respondent of this right to individualized consideration without regard to his race is the principal evil of petitioner's special admissions program.'[17]

Mr. Justice Powell makes this point in the context of an argument (which he accepts) that a university is entitled to take account of race, and other non-academic factors, in pursuit of the educational benefits of a 'good mix' in the student body. But it is plain, especially from his added note, that he regards this matter of individual consideration as a general principle of the highest importance.

The argument on the other side is put succinctly by the four judges who would have ruled in favour of the university and against Bakke. They consider that there is no real difference between giving preference to minority groups by means of a quota and doing so by allowing special weight to minority status in each particular case.

It may be that the Harvard plan is more acceptable to the public than is the Davis 'quota.' . . . But there is no basis for preferring a particular preference program simply because in achieving the same goals that the Davis Medical School is pursuing, it proceeds in a manner that is not immediately apparent to the public.[18]

Did Mr. Justice Powell, then, draw a distinction without a difference? Mr. Justice Brennan and his colleagues, looking at the over-all result, say that there is no difference which counts. There is a difference in public attitude, because the Harvard system conceals the consequences (and intended consequences at that) from overt appearance; but this psychological difference, in the view of the four judges, is not a good reason for saying that the one system, but not the other, conforms to the Constitution. If we are to think of the alleged difference in terms of psychology, however, Mr. Justice Powell's point is better seen in the difference made to the attitude of *applicants*, not of the public. If Allan Bakke had applied to Harvard, he might have been rejected there too, while a black man with lower grades was accepted. But if the two had been considered in competition with each other (it being known that race, among other things, would be taken into account), Bakke would at least have felt that he had had a run for his money; his scholastic record and his personal qualities would have been weighed against the combined qualities of the other candidate. He might still feel that it was unfair to be rejected when his apparent potential for the medical profession was greater than that of the preferred candidate; but at least he would know that he had been considered. Although his rival was given a start in the race, both were allowed to run as competitors.

Looked at in this way, as a question of psychology, the difference is perhaps one of degree. The rejected candidate's feeling of having been unfairly treated is still there, but less strong. Mr. Justice Powell, however, seems to think of the difference as one of kind, as a matter of principle. I agree with him. Concern for collective goals is one thing, concern for the individual is another. Of course, collective goals are intended to benefit groups of individuals, and at some point or other it must be allowed that in a conflict of interests a plurality of individuals count for more than a single individual. Nevertheless, one of the functions of the concept of justice in ethics is to uphold the value of the individual person against the more vaguely conceived value of a collectivity of persons. To be sure, a reference to 'persons' in ordinary speech need not necessarily imply an emphasis on individuality; but in the context of a constitutional provision manifestly designed to secure justice, the Supreme Court's interpretation of 'persons' to mean individuals is virtually inevitable.

But, you may ask, what is the cash value of this alleged difference of kind? What difference does it really make to an Allan Bakke to say that he must be considered as an individual? If the practical *effect* would be the same under the kind of programme used at Harvard, what is the point of claiming for that scheme the virtue of following justice, of treating all applicants as individuals? The point is, I think, that you do not predetermine the result, you leave a genuine option, you give each candidate legitimate room for hope and for such effort as the nature of the competition allows. Even if you can predict of a particular candidate that his chances are not strong, the issue is not foreclosed. This does *not* mean that the difference is one between knowledge and ignorance, that the result is in fact determined but is unknown to the participants. It means that the actual final result can, and sometimes does, turn upon the exercise of initiative by a candidate in the course of the competition procedure, and upon the exercise of reflective choice by those who make the decisions. In short, there is scope for all parties to act as genuine agents. If I am right, Mr. Justice Brennan and his colleagues were mistaken in suggesting that public preference for the Harvard system depends simply on the fact that its results are not 'apparent'.

V

This is a suitable point at which to consider an argument put forward by Professor Ronald Dworkin in favour of reverse discrimination. It is given in a paper which he wrote after the case of DeFunis had been disposed of but before the case of Bakke had come to public attention.[19] The main aim of the paper is to oppose the view that discrimination against DeFunis was unjust and unconstitutional. Broadly speaking, Dworkin agrees with the submissions later made on behalf of the Davis Medical School in *Bakke* to the effect that a highly desirable social goal can, in certain circumstances, outweigh the right of an individual.

At first sight it seems odd that Dworkin should take this position, because in general he holds that rights are more important than social goals. In publishing a number of his essays, including this paper on 'Reverse Discrimination', as a book, he picked out the title of one, 'Taking Rights Seriously', to serve as the title of the whole volume; and in the Introduction to the book he said that his aim was to criticize legal positivism and utilitarianism and to put in their place a theory of 'individual human rights'. But in 'Reverse Discrimination' he argues that an important social goal can outweigh an individual right. 'An individual's right to be treated as an equal means that his potential loss must be treated as a matter of concern, but that loss may nevertheless be outweighed by the gain to the community as a whole.'[20] That sentence at least seems to lend support to utilitarianism, and to the utilitarian view of rights as matters of gain and loss to be weighed in the balance of gain and loss 'to the community as a whole'. At the end of the article Dworkin claims that his arguments in favour of reverse discrimination are 'both utilitarian and ideal'. The ideal argument, he says, is that 'a more equal society is a better society'[21] (or 'more just').[22] So his view is that the individual right of a DeFunis can be outweighed either by an increase of gain to the community or by an increase of goodness or justice in the community, the latter increase taking place through a decrease in inequality.

According to Dworkin, the susceptibility of a right to be outweighed by a social goal is subject to two qualifications. (1) So far as utilitarian (or 'economic') goals are concerned, the gain to the community which may be placed in the balance must not include

such gain as is morally improper, e.g. the satisfaction of prejudice.
(2) If a social policy violates a 'distinct right', then 'the fact that the
policy might achieve an overall social gain would not justify the
violation'. That is how he states the matter in *Taking Rights
Seriously*.[23] In *Philosophical Law*[24] the second qualification is re-
phrased into talk about 'rights so important' that they must be
respected 'even at the cost of policy', but later on[25] Dworkin
reverts to his earlier form of expression about 'any distinct independent right'. I think these variations show that he is unsure of
his ground.

I am not concerned with the first qualification, concerning the
kind of social gain which may or may not be counted in the scale.
Dworkin explains it with a peculiar interpretation of utilitarianism
in terms of preferences, some of which are 'internal' (i.e. concerned
with benefits to the person expressing the preference), others
'external' (i.e. concerned with benefits to persons other than the
one expressing the preference). I think that in fact this interpretation of utilitarianism is misconceived and unrealistic (all the more
misconceived because Dworkin first introduces preferences as giving a more practical method of utilitarian judgement than does an
attempted calculation of public benefit). But this criticism does not
affect the principle of Dworkin's conclusion. A genuine utilitarian
would agree with Dworkin that the satisfaction of a prejudice
should not count as an addition to public gain, but he would do so
on the ground that the *total* consequences of satisfying prejudice
contain more harm than benefit.

My concern here, however, is with Dworkin's second qualification, about the character of rights that cannot (morally) be outweighed by a social goal. In some places Dworkin suggests that
such a right is a 'distinct' right, in others that it is an 'important'
right or even an 'absolute' right.[26]

Reference to a 'distinct right' is relevant only in terms of the
U.S. Constitution. Dworkin's point is that the Equal Protection
Clause of the Fourteenth Amendment does not itself contain an
explicit prohibition of discrimination in terms that clearly apply to
educational institutions. The clause has been interpreted in that
way by the Supreme Court in recent decades, but earlier judges of
the Supreme Court had been content to tolerate, for example,
separate schools and colleges for blacks. Dworkin contrasts with

this the 'distinct' rights to freedom of speech and freedom of religion. He presumably has in mind the First Amendment. When it declares that Congress shall make no law abridging freedom of speech or of the press, this certainly means that the U.S. Congress cannot, as the British Parliament can, enact a statute limiting such freedom. But does it really imply that freedom of expression can *never* be limited in the United States if the national interest appears to require it, e.g. in time of war? That would be very surprising. I gather that in fact censorship has been exercised by indirect means such as administrative acts. The same sort of consideration applies to Dworkin's second example of a distinct right, freedom of religion. The First Amendment also forbids Congress to make any law establishing religion or prohibiting the free exercise of it. Suppose some group of people in the United States were to institute a religion that required human sacrifice. Does anyone imagine that such a religion would be tolerated, even though Congress could not, under the Constitution, enact a statute prohibiting it?

The specification in the U.S. Constitution of distinct rights in respect of freedom of expression and freedom of religion is due to particular historical circumstances. It is true that the U.S. Constitution does not similarly specify a distinct right to non-discrimination in education (although one can say, as against this, that the provision of the California Constitution which Bakke invoked is relatively specific, and that the *statutory* right set up by the Civil Rights Act of 1964 is very distinctive and clearly applies to educational institutions in receipt of Federal funds). The early history of the United States brought into prominence the demand to protect freedom of religion and freedom of expression. But it is perfectly possible that, in a hundred years from now, a majority of people in the United States (and in other western societies) will think little of being able to practise the religion of their choice, but much of being able to train for the profession of their choice. In those circumstances, they would regard the right to compete freely, in terms of ability, for entry to a Medical or Law School, as more important than the right to follow religious practices. Any argument that the latter was still a 'distinct' right in the U.S. Constitution, while the former was not, would leave them cold.

However, Dworkin would probably agree that the issue between the advocates and the critics of reverse discrimination is one of ethics in any liberal society, and not just one of constitutional law in the United States. It seems to me quite clear that no right can be immune in all circumstances from having to give way to social policy. Like Dworkin in his better moments (and unlike Dworkin in that sentence about counting the violation of an individual right as a 'loss' to be outweighed by social 'gain'), I think that individual rights are more of a barrier to social policy than are interests which are not incorporated into rights. Very often policy ought to give way to firm rights, even though the balance of advantage lies with policy. But it cannot be true that the interest of the community must *always*, even in the most dire straits, have a lesser moral claim than the rights of an individual.

This brings me to the second category of rights which Dworkin seems to consider invincible by social policy. As I have mentioned, he speaks of them as rights 'so important' as to outweigh policy, but also as 'absolute' rights. His examples are: the right that the State provide a man with shelter if he cannot afford it himself,[27] and (this one is expressed as a possibility only) the 'right to equal treatment in elementary education, because someone who is denied elementary education is unlikely to lead a useful life.'[28] The examples suggest that Dworkin is thinking about basic or fundamental rights, rights to facilities the lack of which makes life intolerable. No one will dispute his view that the right to shelter and the right to elementary education are more important than the right to compete on equal terms for entry to higher education. But can one elicit from this some point of principle, to the effect that such fundamental rights are absolute and can never be outweighed by social policy? I think not. No right can be absolute, if only because any right of any one individual is susceptible of conflicting with a similar right of some other individual. This means that they cannot both be satisfied and so cannot be absolute. It may be said that a right might be absolute against social policy although not against the right of another individual. But this distinction cannot be sustained so as to defend absolute rights. Take Dworkin's example of an individual's right to be sheltered by the State if he cannot afford to shelter himself. What if the State cannot afford it either? Suppose there has been a natural disaster, or a terrible war, with the result that there are many unfortunates without shelter and not enough buildings to house them? Suppose, too, that the diversion of the meagre remaining resources of the State to providing more shelter will mean neglecting to provide food for other unfortunates, who will then starve. It is immaterial whether you say that this is a conflict of rights against rights, or a conflict of rights against a social goal. In critical circumstances a social goal can be identical with a collection of rights.

This is not to argue that social goals can *always* be analysed as equivalent to a collection of rights. There are two reasons why they cannot. First, while all social goals that deserve the name will benefit individuals when they are realized, those effects are too indistinct in the original conception to allow us generally to equate social goals with a collection of the interests of actual individuals. And secondly, even if that equation were proper, not all interests are of sufficient urgency or importance to be counted as rights, as imposing obligations upon others.

What I have said of the right to shelter is *a fortiori* true of the somewhat less fundamental right to elementary education. I do not agree with Dworkin that, without elementary education, people are unlikely to lead a useful life. He should look around a little more widely, both in space and in time. Universal elementary education is a relatively recent phenomenon. Apart from easily ascertained facts of history and geography, I can appeal to personal experience, even in England in my lifetime. When I was young I knew many immigrants (including my own parents) who had received no secular education at all; but most of them lived useful and fairly happy lives. Of course I agree that elementary education is an enormous help towards living a useful life, and I entirely agree that in the modern world it should be regarded as a fundamental moral right. But it is certainly not of absolute validity against all other social policies. If it conflicted with the social goal of providing for even more basic needs, food and shelter, for example, it would have to give way.

If no rights are immune from ever being outweighed by social goals, it follows that there is no absolute bar to reverse discrimination. But one does need to be rather wary of Dworkin's method of justifying it. I am not at all sure that the straightforward utilitarian goal of maximizing the *general* interest can have the moral weight required to overrule an individual's right not to be discriminated against by a public body. In fact I rather think that many utilitarians would say that such discrimination is to be condemned on grounds of utility itself, because the indirect consequences of reverse discrimination are harmful to the general interest. My own view, however, is non-utilitarian. If reverse discrimination is to be justified, the case must be made in terms of what the policy will do, and what the community owes, to the disadvantaged group whom it is now proposed to favour. The case cannot be made in terms of what the policy will do for society as a whole. However, there is perhaps room for difference of opinion here.

Far more questionable is Dworkin's 'ideal argument', the suggestion that a more equal society is a 'better' or a 'more just' society than an unequal one, and that therefore the social goal of producing an equal society can override the rights of individuals not to be subject to reverse discrimination. The only sound argument for equalitarianism that I can find is based on the fact that nearly all human beings share with each other, but not with other animals, certain capacities and needs which are of the greatest importance to them. This fact justifies imputing a certain equality of rights to all human beings—as individuals. It does not justify an equal *society* in the abstract. I can see the sense of claiming various kinds of equality for individual persons, and of treating that claim as an important part of the concept of justice. But I cannot see the sense of saying that an equal *society* is better, or more just, than an unequal society. Would a family be a 'better' community if parents and children of all ages had equal authority and equal rights to use resources? Would a society be 'more just' if equal facilities were provided for those in need and those not in need, or if equal recompense were given to the industrious and the idle, equal respect to the benevolent and the selfish? Reverse discrimination in favour of a disadvantaged minority can be supported on the ground of seeking to give equality of rights *to that minority*. It is quite irrelevant to say that the policy will produce an equal *society*.

vi

A community has an obligation of justice to remove unmerited disadvantages from individual members or particular groups. The American community has a specially weighty obligation in relation to American blacks because of the history of slavery in their country. This is what counted above all in leading Justices Brennan, White, Marshall, and Blackmun, in the Bakke case, to an opinion in favour of the Davis Medical School. The essence of their view is shown in a rhetorical flourish near the beginning of their judgement:

Our Nation was founded on the principle that 'all men are created equal'. Yet candor requires acknowledgment that the Framers of our Constitution, to forge the Thirteen Colonies into one Nation, openly compromised this principle of equality with its antithesis: slavery. The consequences of this compromise are well known and have aptly been called our 'American Dilemma.'[29]

All reflective Americans would agree that they therefore have a special obligation of redress. But on whom is the burden of redress to fall? If it falls, by and large, on the whole of the white section of the community, requiring from most of them some financial loss or some sacrifice of amenity or opportunity, that is fair enough. But when the sacrifice has to be borne by a few individuals, such as DeFunis and Bakke, a further issue of justice arises. In the Bakke case, Mr. Justice Powell put it like this: 'there is a measure of inequity in forcing innocent persons in respondent's position to bear the burdens of redressing grievances not of their making.'[30] One may say that all, or practically all, present-day Americans are equally innocent of the wrongs done to American blacks by the American past, and that there is a measure of inequity in asking them, as a body, 'to bear the burdens of redressing grievances not of their making'. True, but if the burdens have to be borne somewhere, then there is a measure of very rough but realistic justice in accepting that the sins of the fathers shall be visited upon the children. There is not even the roughest of justice, however, in allowing the burden to fall upon the shoulders of a few isolated individuals. On the contrary, it is a very plain injustice and is apt to strike those affected as a very harsh injustice.

The force of this point was not lost upon one, at least, of the judges who favoured the Davis Medical School. Mr. Justice Blackmun wrote a short additional judgement in which he acknowledged that 'Allan Bakke is not himself charged with discrimination and yet is the one who is disadvantaged'.[31] As he went on to observe, the problem would not exist if the number of places in Graduate Schools were expanded to meet the demand from all qualified applicants; but this would be neither feasible, because the resources are not available, nor justifiable, because there is no clear need for such increased numbers of doctors, lawyers, and other products of the Graduate Schools. Issues of distributive justice arise when there is a scarcity of benefits for an excess of potential beneficiaries. Some claimants have to be given priority, and the question is what criteria should be used to select them. The criteria that appear to be most obviously relevant, from a moral point of view, are need and merit. In the absence of any clear difference in need or merit as between two or more candidates—i.e. if their needs or merits appear to be roughly equal—they should be treated equally. If the need of one is greater than that of another, the first should be preferred. Likewise if the merit of one is greater than that of another. But how is need to be weighed against merit? There is no straightforward answer to that question. If the need is a vital need (as when food or medical care is needed to prevent death or chronic disablement), we shall all agree that it takes priority over requiting merit with benefits which are desirable but not essential. Where, however, the need itself falls into the category of the desirable rather than the essential (and so is a want or a lack rather than a need, strictly speaking), there seems no reason, in terms of justice, to give it priority over merit; and in terms of social utility the claim of merit has the greater weight.

How does reverse discrimination stand in relation to these distinctions? Sometimes the case for reverse discrimination does aim at meeting a fairly basic need of members of a disadvantaged minority. For example, employers of any sizeable enterprise may be required by law to appoint disabled persons to not less than some (small) fixed percentage of their labour force. In the United States it would generally be regarded as perfectly proper to make the same requirement for the employment of minority ethnic groups. A law of this kind lays down a quota. The need that it meets is not literally vital; a job is not essential for life, in a modern civilized society. But it is commonly thought to be essential for a decent human life. Equally relevant is the fact that such a quota will not be imposed if it is likely to produce actual unemployment for members of the non-disadvantaged majority. The assumption is that the majority do not have the desperate difficulty in getting a job that faces the disadvantaged minority. The need of the minority is clearly greater than that of the majority.

Reverse discrimination for admission to professional training is a different matter. To become a doctor is not an essential need either for Allan Bakke or for the less talented applicants from minority ethnic groups who were given places under the Davis quota system. The case for reverse discrimination is that the minority ethnic *communities*, especially the black communities, will be benefited if there are more black doctors, both because (so it is claimed) black doctors will be more likely than white doctors to serve in black communities, and because an increase of blacks in the medical and other professions will encourage young blacks of ability to apply for training. The first of these reasons can be, and has been, doubted, but it is a fair point to make, as is the second. However, this case for reverse discrimination is more one of utility than of justice. It will be useful for the black communities if there are more black doctors, since that is likely to mean more doctors in black communities. It will be useful for the society as a whole if there are more black doctors, since that is likely to raise the general standard of entry to the medical profession by encouraging applications from many able young people who at present do not apply. The policy will also be useful for the individual applicants, on the reasonable assumption that a person who has the ability to become a doctor is likely to find satisfaction and fulfilment in the practice of medicine; but then this will be true of any applicants of ability, whatever ethnic group they come from. Is there any issue of justice to individuals, or of individual rights, which is better satisfied by the policy of reverse discrimination than by its absence? Not that I can see. There is the legitimate point that reverse discrimination attempts to redress past injustice to the minority *group*. But so far as justice to *individuals* is concerned, the exclusion of Bakke, in order to make up for the sins of others in the past, is a clear injustice; while it is not an injustice to an individual black applicant to reject him in favour of Bakke on the ground that Bakke has the lead in the qualities that indicate capacity for becoming a good doctor. Can the claim of justice for a group legitimate injustice to an individual? Some people will say so, including people in communist countries who give more attention to the interests of groups, such as social classes, than to the rights of individuals; hence the prevalence, in such countries, of reverse discrimination in higher education for the sake of

L

increasing the proportion of students who are the children of manual workers. To someone imbued with the liberal tradition of valuing the individual person, it does not seem right.

The dilemmas of justice, the conflicts between different claims of justice, or between claims of justice and the values of social utility, do not admit of clear resolution in only one way. As I have just indicated, different political traditions lead people to evaluate differently the competing claims. Even within a more or less single political tradition, the different histories of different societies will lead to different evaluations. In the United States, practically all reflective people agree that some kind of reverse discrimination in entry to higher education is justified; they are divided on whether a quota system is legitimate. In Britain, I think, very few people indeed would countenance a quota system, and a substantial majority would question the propriety even of less blatant systems of reverse discrimination. They would all accept discrimination on grounds of desert, e.g. in favour of ex-servicemen after a war; but not on the simple ground of belonging to a disadvantaged group.

The difference lies in history. Reflective people in Britain may well think that our forebears were guilty of exploitation of colonial peoples and that we therefore have a special obligation to give them aid towards the economic development of their countries. Where individuals from such countries have been encouraged to come to Britain at a time of labour shortage, we have a special obligation to help them and their children to integrate into our society, and this may call for discriminatory expenditure in regard to schools, housing, and employment. The costs in both types of instance will fall upon the community at large. There will be none of the obvious injustice which comes from fastening a sacrifice upon particular individuals. There is no need for this; and if a proposed policy did have such a consequence, I think there would be strong opposition to it on the ground of injustice. But then there is simply no comparison between our obligations to, e.g., West Indians in Britain and the obligations of American whites to American blacks. A number of West Indians were encouraged to come to Britain in the years after the Second World War to take jobs in nursing and transport; but they did after all have a free choice. Other immigrants from former British dependencies have come here entirely of their own free will, preferring the opportunities (and the risks) of life in Britain to a dismal economic situation in their (now independent) native lands. The American Negroes had no choice. They were forcibly taken to America, lived as slaves with severely limited rights, and after emancipation had to fight hard for equal opportunities even in the north, to say nothing of their infinitely harder task in the south. Now that the conscience of the U.S.A. has been sufficiently stirred to take effective steps towards resolving the 'American dilemma', many liberals are prepared to compromise their traditional principles so as to allow injustice to individuals for the sake of advancement for blacks.

The opinion of the four judges in the Bakke case who favoured the Davis Medical School was chiefly influenced by reflection on the history of blacks in America. This suggests that they would have been far less ready to countenance such a system of reverse discrimination if it had worked so as to favour other ethnic minorities only. Suppose, for example, that there were a scarcity of places in courses that for some reason did not appeal to blacks but did appeal to Asians and Chicanos. This could conceivably be true of courses in foreign languages. The claims and the difficulties of Asians and Chicanos would be similar to those of immigrants in Britain. Of course it would be virtually impossible to make a distinction of principle between these courses and others in the one country. But if the problems of blacks in America had not brought up any difficulties about university entrance, and if there were this difficulty about university entrance for Asians and Chicanos, I doubt very much whether so many American liberals, and four judges of the Supreme Court, would have favoured a quota system of reverse discrimination—or perhaps any system of reverse discrimination.

One interesting thing about the Bakke case is that a good many American liberals, while supporting some form of reverse discrimination in order to advance the cause of blacks, were not prepared to let this override their traditional principles of justice for individuals. It shows that those principles have a strength for the liberal conscience which can stand out even against the very proper sentiment of wanting justice for blacks as a group. I do not say that they are right and their opponents are wrong. The dilemmas of justice are conflicts of right against right, and I do not see any objective way of deciding that one of the conflicting claims has more right about it than the other. It does seem to be a fact, however, that a substantial proportion of reflective Americans stands on each side of the dispute. If so, the judgement of the Supreme Court in the Bakke case, far from being confusing, is a fair and accurate picture of the divided conscience of America. Whether majority opinion in the country (among reflective people) would be on the same side as the majority opinion in the court, I do not know.[32] But the mere fact that there are the two, firmly and widely held, opposing opinions in the country is a very good reason for welcoming the decision of the court in allowing a limited form of reverse discrimination and forbidding any programme which results in blatant injustice to particular individuals.

i

The subject of this essay is historical but the philosophical problem with which it is concerned is a continuing one. The chief difficulty that faces utilitarianism as a theory of ethics is to show that it can give an adequate account of the concept of justice. This was clearly seen and honestly faced by J. S. Mill, Sidgwick, and Rashdall. Mill and Rashdall thought they could accommodate justice within a strictly utilitarian theory, but to my mind their arguments are faulty. Sidgwick acknowledged that utilitarian principles alone are inadequate and added a separate principle of equity.

Most of us find an immediate attraction in utilitarianism. If we are later convinced that it does not account satisfactorily for the concept of justice, we are not quite sure which way to go. In the history of ideas the utilitarian tradition has been opposed to the natural law tradition, and in general (though not universally) natural law theory has gone along with a form of rationalism, while utilitarianism has gone along with empiricism. Rationalism is out of fashion, and so one is disinclined to talk about principles of justice evident to rational intuition. I do not know if this partly explains why Professor John Rawls, having decided that a utilitarian account of justice will not do, has put forward an account of justice in terms of social contract theory. He says in one of his papers that the social contract is the traditional opponent of utilitarianism and so is the obvious alternative to it. I think he is mistaken. The theory of social contract was intended to deal with the problem of political obligation (why should a man obey the State?), not as an explanation of justice. However that may be, I find the contractual hypothesis in Rawls's theory singularly unhelpful, although his book, taken as a whole, is clearly an important contribution to ethical theory. Nevertheless I am no more inclined than the next man to revert to intuitionism, even though the clearest-headed of the utilitarians, Sidgwick, did so. Like most people nowadays, I want to stick to empiricism as far as I can. The best empiricist approaches to the concept of justice that I know are those of Hume and Adam Smith. Hume is by and large a utilitarian. Adam Smith is an anti-utilitarian, indeed a natural law theorist, but his natural law is natural law with a difference, a genuinely empiricist natural law.

Both Hume and Adam Smith were strongly influenced by Francis Hutcheson. Smith was a pupil of Hutcheson and shared his interests in ethics, aesthetics, law, and economics. Hume's relation to Hutcheson is more complex. Hume's ethical theory was a development of Hutcheson's, showing greater insight and greater subtlety. But that is not the whole of the story. Unlike Hutcheson and Adam Smith, Hume was more deeply interested in the philosophy of knowledge than in the philosophy of practice, and it was in the theory of knowledge that he displayed outstanding genius as a philosopher of the first rank. Kemp Smith[1] has shown, I think conclusively, that although Hume wrote and published Book III of the *Treatise of Human Nature* later than Books I and II, he began his philosophizing with ethics—Hutcheson's ethics—and was led by that to think he had the key to the problems of knowledge. Hutcheson treated beauty and virtue as partly projections of the feelings of spectators. What Hume did was to apply the same sort of move to ideas which were troublesome in the theory of knowledge. His genius lay in seeing that the move could be so applied more generally (as well as in the remorseless logic of his criticism of alternative accounts), and the greatness of his achievement is not diminished when we perceive that he took the initial idea from Hutcheson.

I do not know whether one can properly say that Hutcheson was the first utilitarian. A good case can be made for holding that Richard Cumberland, a traditional natural law theorist of the seventeenth century, had a utilitarian theory of ethics. But Hutcheson was more explicitly utilitarian, and—what is more to the point—he was the first thinker to produce a utilitarian theory from clearly empiricist foundations.

Hutcheson was of course also an exponent (as Hume was after him) of the moral sense theory. In the hands of Hutcheson the moral sense theory turned into utilitarianism in the following way. He began by insisting, against Hobbes and Mandeville, that there are disinterested factors in human psychology. There is disinterested love (affection, admiration) and disinterested dislike. We see these things not only in ethics, which some would dispute, but also in aesthetics, which is harder to deny. There is a disinterested motive to action, benevolence; and when a man acts from this disinterested motive, spectators naturally feel a disinterested approval analogous to the disinterested liking felt by spectators of natural beauty and art. The capacity to feel approval or disapproval is the moral sense. Virtue for Hutcheson is *benevolence approved*, not benevolence on its own, but benevolence as seen in the eye of the beholder (or, more properly, as felt in the heart of the beholder). That is the gist of the moral sense theory.

But now: benevolence aims at giving happiness to others (or removing their misery), and while it does not always succeed it commonly does so. Therefore the tendency, and the aim, of virtuous action is the promotion of happiness for people in general (indeed for any sensitive creature). Although the feeling of the moral sense is an immediate reaction, not a calculated one, a wide benevolence is approved more than a narrow, and a universal benevolence is approved most of all. So on reflection we can see a correlation between the strength of approval and the degree to which the approved agent intends to increase and spread happiness. Hence Hutcheson concluded that 'that action is best which procures the greatest happiness for the greatest numbers'.

All virtue for Hutcheson is a form of benevolence, a natural motive to which there is a natural reaction. Hutcheson treated any virtue that aims at benefiting other people (e.g. gratitude) as a form of benevolence. He denied that prudence is a virtue except to the extent that it enables us to exercise benevolence. He apparently did not feel any tension between benevolence and justice, and he defined rights in terms of universal practices that would promote or harm general happiness. Note that the account is in terms of *universal* practices. This is because Hutcheson was thinking of the rules of law when he talked about rights.

In Hume's development of Hutcheson's theory of ethics there are three things especially worthy of notice. (1) Like Hutcheson, Hume supported a theory of moral sense or sentiment by criticizing rationalist alternatives, but in Hume the attack on ethical rationalism was conducted with a battery of arguments as powerful

as any in the history of philosophy. (2) Where Hutcheson had taken
the moral sense to be a basic datum of human psychology, Hume
explained it as an effect of sympathy. He thereby made it seem less
mysterious and showed up more clearly the connection between the
moral sense theory and utilitarianism. We feel a particular form of
pleasure (approval) when we see a benevolent action, because we
share by sympathy the pleasure of the beneficiary of the benevolent
action; and likewise disapproval arises from sympathy with pain or
distress caused by a vicious action. (3) Hume distinguished between benevolence and justice as 'natural' and 'artificial' virtues
respectively, and recognized that the moral approval of justice
requires further explanation. It is the third feature with which I
am especially concerned here.

Hume's presentation of his view of justice differs markedly in
the *Treatise* and in the *Enquiry concerning the Principles of Morals*.
In the *Treatise* he stressed the thesis that justice is an artificial
virtue, one that arises from human conventions. By denying that
it is a natural virtue, Hume meant that the motive for acting justly
is not a basic endowment of human nature, as e.g. benevolence is.
When Hume talked about justice he was generally thinking of rules
about property. These are needed, he argued, because there is a
scarcity in the supply of many goods that are wanted and because
men are predominantly selfish with limited generosity. In a
fictitious golden age or utopian state of nature, in which the supply
of desired goods and the extent of human benevolence were unlimited, there would be no need for rules of mine and thine. As
things are, however, we all find it advantageous to follow conventions of leaving others in undisturbed possession of goods so long
as they do the same for us. And so there arise rules for 'stability'
of possession. A man's first motive for joining in the conventions
is self-interest. But how explain the fact that we morally approve
of keeping the rules even in instances which do not benefit us?
Hume's explanation was that we see that the system of rules as a
whole is of benefit to society in general, and sympathy with the
public interest gives rise to moral approval. In the *Treatise* Hume
acknowledged that 'a single act of justice is frequently contrary to
public interest',[2] let alone private. But the whole system is
advantageous, both to the public at large and to each individual
considered by himself; and Hume argued that an essential feature

of the system is that the rules be followed inflexibly in every instance. Without this rigidity, he thought, the system would collapse.

One may be sceptical of these last remarks, but the point to note at the moment is that in the *Treatise* Hume was aware of a problem in subsuming justice under utility. He recognized that on occasion (he himself said 'frequently') particular acts of justice are contrary to public interest. He also recognized, at the beginning of his discussion,

> that men, in the ordinary conduct of life, look not so far as the public interest, when they pay their creditors, perform their promises, and abstain from theft, and robbery, and injustice of every kind. That is a motive too remote and too sublime to affect the generality of mankind, and operate with any force in actions so contrary to private interest as are frequently those of justice and common honesty.[3]

If I am not mistaken, Hume's view in the *Treatise* was that a moral approbation for the rules of justice arises from sympathy with the public interest which these rules normally serve, and that this feeling of moral approbation becomes attached by association of ideas to all instances of keeping the rules, even when their contribution to public interest is not obvious and so cannot produce sympathy.

In the *Enquiry* Hume's position was simpler, and to my mind less satisfactory. I suppose that his insistence in the *Treatise* on the artificial nature of justice was intended as a rejection of Locke's view that there is a natural right to property. Locke was to a large extent a rationalist and a traditional natural law man in ethics. So in Hume's mind the general attack on ethical rationalism, with which the *Treatise* began, could be made more specific by an attack on the idea that property is founded on natural right. Accordingly, in Book III of the *Treatise* he first argued against rationalism and in favour of a moral sense; then in part ii he dealt with justice, stressing its artificial character; and finally in part iii he considered the natural virtues, including benevolence. When Hume came to write the *Enquiry*, he virtually dropped the thesis that justice is artificial, saying that dispute on this question was purely verbal; he relegated the dispute about reason and sense (or sentiment) to an appendix; and after an introductory section his order of treatment was to discuss benevolence first, to take justice and government next, and then to elaborate the relation of all the virtues to the useful and the agreeable. Either Hume had now lost interest in attacking rationalism, or he felt that rationalists could never be roused from their dogmatic slumber, or (the most probable hypothesis) he thought that he would get a wider reading public if he highlighted those parts of his theory that were more intelligible to laymen. At any rate the discussion of justice in the *Enquiry* was directed to show that justice is *wholly* founded on utility while benevolence is only partly so. The main argument for the conclusion was as before: relative scarcity of goods and limited generosity make justice necessary for the benefit of human life. In a utopia of plenty, or one of unlimited altruism, there would be no rules of justice because they would be useless. Again, in the converse conditions of extreme scarcity or of extreme self-regard (as in a Hobbesian state of nature or a state of war), the rules of justice are suspended because there too they are useless.

The writing is splendid and justifies, as a *literary* judgement, Hume's statement in *My Own Life* that of all his works the *Enquiry concerning the Principles of Morals* was 'incomparably the best'. But how does it stand philosophically? One is given the impression that justice fits a utilitarian account of ethics more completely than does benevolence. Can that possibly be true? Hume mentioned the difficulties but was too cursory with them. In appendix iii, noting that particular acts of justice may be harmful to the public interest, he said 'it follows that every man, in embracing that virtue, must have an eye to the whole plan or system'.[4] What price now the statement of the *Treatise* which I quoted earlier?

> Experience sufficiently proves, that men, in the ordinary conduct of life, look not so far as the public interest, when they pay their creditors, perform their promises, and abstain from theft, and robbery, and injustice of every kind. That is a motive too remote and too sublime to affect the generality of mankind . . .

Hume's discussion of justice concentrated on laws of property, and on *civil* rather than *criminal* law (as we can see from his sections in the *Treatise* about the different methods of acquiring a title to property).

Adam Smith on the contrary had the criminal law chiefly in mind when, in an early part of the *Theory of Moral Sentiments* (II.ii.3), he considered the relation of justice to utility. (In his *Lectures on Jurisprudence* he touched on the question when discussing property rights as well as repeating the *Moral Sentiments* view about the justice of punishment.) In the *Moral Sentiments* Smith's account of justice followed immediately upon his account of merit. Like Hume in the *Treatise*, Adam Smith made sympathy basic to his ethical theory. But the concept of sympathy which he used is different from Hume's, indeed more subtle and having more explanatory power.

Smith began with the 'sense of propriety' (i.e. the judgement that something is right). Hume held that moral approval and disapproval result from sympathy with people who are *affected* by the action judged. A benevolent action normally has the consequence of giving happiness. We sympathize with the beneficiary and so approve of the action. Smith instead looked in the first instance to sympathy with the feelings of the *agent*. As a spectator I imagine myself in the agent's shoes. If I find that I should be moved to act as he does in that situation, then my observation of the correspondence between his feelings ('sentiments') and my own hypothetical feelings is an observation of 'sympathy'. This observation of correspondence of sentiments causes me to approve of the agent's motive, to think of it as 'appropriate' or 'proper'.

But then, when I also note the feelings of the person affected by the action, there can be a second sympathy. Let us suppose that B (the beneficiary) is in need and that A (the agent) is moved to help him. As a spectator I sympathize with A's motive of benevolence and I approve of it as proper. B feels grateful to A. I can imagine myself in B's shoes, too, and I find that I likewise would feel grateful; so I approve of B's feelings as appropriate. The conjunction of the *two* sympathies gives rise to the 'sense of merit'. An impartial spectator will sympathize with B's gratitude, and so think it proper, only if he also thinks A's action is proper. When he does have this double sympathy, he judges A's action to be meritorious, i.e. to deserve the gratitude of B and the kind of action that gratitude motivates, doing good in return.

Contrariwise, if A harms B, B is liable to feel resentment. An impartial spectator will sympathize with B's resentment only if he also thinks that A's action was improper, i.e. if he feels an antipathy instead of a sympathy for A's motive. If he sympathizes with A because he thinks that A's harmful action was justified, he will not sympathize with B's resentment. But if he does think that B's resentment is proper and A's action improper, he will judge A's action to have demerit, i.e. to deserve resentment and the kind of action that resentment motivates, a retaliation of harm.

It was from this point that Adam Smith moved on to the distinction between justice and beneficence. Acts of beneficence, if done from proper motives, deserve reward, being the proper objects of gratitude. Harmful acts, if done from improper motives, deserve punishment, being the proper objects of resentment. Smith thought of justice as primarily requiring us to refrain from harming others. The mere lack of beneficence, so long as it does no positive harm, does not call for punishment. Beneficence differs from justice therefore in being 'free', i.e. in not being enforceable by the threat of punishment. Justice is enforceable, attended by sanctions. Retaliation is a law of nature, both the returning of good for good, and the returning of harm for harm. Where resentment and the retaliation of harm for harm would be approved by an impartial spectator, there punishment is in order.

When Smith came to consider the relation of justice to utility, he conceded quite a lot to Hume, indeed perhaps too much. (I think there is no doubt that he had Hume chiefly in mind when he wrote this particular chapter of the *Theory of Moral Sentiments*.) He agreed that the social utility of justice is greater than that of beneficence in that justice is essential to the existence of society. But, he argued, this does not imply that approval of justice arises from the thought of its utility. To suppose otherwise is to confuse final and efficient causation, or (as people would put the point today) it is to confuse function with cause. Justice has the function of preserving society, but this does not mean that men establish, follow, and approve the set of practices called just because they see its utility. The thought of social utility is often a secondary consideration confirming our natural feeling of what is proper and merited. It is, however, seldom the first consideration.

All men, even the most stupid and unthinking, abhor fraud, perfidy, and injustice, and delight to see them punished. But few men have reflected upon the necessity of justice to the existence of society, how obvious soever that necessity may appear to be.[5]

Our concern for an individual does not depend on a concern for the society of which he forms a part, any more than our concern for the loss of a guinea depends on the thought that it forms part of a fortune of a thousand guineas. On the contrary, our regard for a multitude is made up of particular regards for the individual members of the multitude.

Smith allowed that there are some exceptional instances where the application and the approval of punishment depend purely on social utility, and he argued that the exceptions prove the rule because our attitude is clearly different in the exceptional and in the normal instance. As an example of the exceptions he cited the case of a sentinel in the army who was put to death for falling asleep at his post. It was a real life case, which evidently impressed Smith very much by the conflicting feelings to which it gave rise in him as a typical spectator. He referred to it in the *Moral Sentiments*, in a fragment of a lecture on justice which happens to be preserved in Glasgow University Library, and in his Lectures on Jurisprudence. A crime like that of the sentinel, said Smith, does not directly harm any individual, but it is thought to be actually or potentially harmful to society in its remote consequences. The severity of the punishment may seem to be necessary and for that reason 'just and proper'. Yet, although justified by utility, the punishment appears 'excessively severe'. 'The natural atrocity of the crime seems to be so little, and the punishment so great, that it is with great difficulty that our heart can reconcile itself to it.' The punishment does not fit the crime in terms of desert. 'A man of humanity' has to make an effort to approve of it. Things are quite different when the man of humanity contemplates a similar punishment for 'an ungrateful murderer or parricide'. There he readily applauds the 'just retaliation'.

The very different sentiments with which the spectator views those different punishments, is a proof that his approbation of the one is far from being founded upon the same principles with that of the other. He looks upon the sentinel as an unfortunate victim, who, indeed, must and ought to be devoted to the safety of numbers, but whom still, in his heart, he would be glad to save; and he is only sorry that the interest of the many should oppose it. But if the murderer should escape from punishment, it would excite his highest indignation . . .[6]

In his Lectures on Jurisprudence Smith preceded the example of the sentinel with another, which he evidently thought more telling. Because wool was considered the main source of national wealth in England, a statute in the reign of Charles II prohibited the export of wool on pain of death.

Yet tho' wool was exported as formerly and men were convinced that the practice was pernicious, no jury, no evidence, could be got against the offenders. The exportation of wool is naturaly no crime, and men could not be brought to consider it as punishable with death.[7]

When Smith said it is 'naturaly no crime', he meant it is not the sort of thing that naturally excites sympathy with resentment at injury.

I said earlier that Smith perhaps conceded too much to Hume in the *Moral Sentiments* chapter. He was too ready to agree that *justification* on grounds of utility makes an act *just*. He said that the execution of the sentinel is not only proper but also just. He did not say this, in the Jurisprudence Lectures, of the death penalty for exporting wool. Men were agreed that the export of wool was socially pernicious but they did not consider the penalty proper, let alone just. In the *Moral Sentiments* Smith said of the sentinel: 'When the preservation of an individual is inconsistent with the safety of a multitude, nothing can be more just than that the many should be preferred to the one.' In the fragmentary manuscript of his lecture on justice, written earlier than the *Moral Sentiments*, he had similarly said: 'Nothing can be more just, than that one man should be sacrificed to the security of thousands.' But towards the end of the lecture he added something else which is inconsistent with this. 'Improper punishment, punishment which is either not due at all or which exceeds the demerit of the crime, is an injury to the criminal . . .' Now since, as the *Moral Sentiments* put it, the punishment of the sentinel 'appears to be excessively severe', for 'the natural atrocity of the crime seems to be so little, and the punishment so great', it is punishment 'which exceeds the demerit of the crime' and is therefore 'an injury to the criminal'. That which does an injury is unjust. It may still be warranted as right and proper on the grounds of a degree of utility great enough to override the injustice, but *unjust* it remains. The sentinel is an 'unfortunate victim' who must be 'devoted to the safety of numbers'. The example of the export of wool is simpler and less instructive, though in a sense more telling for Smith's case against utilitarianism, because in that example the refusal of witnesses to give evidence and of juries to convict means that they regarded the claim of utility as overridden by that of justice.

ii

It is worth recalling two features of these accounts of justice given by Hume and Smith. (1) Both men conducted their discussions in the light of the actual working of the law. They were writing in a tradition in which moral philosophy included jurisprudence as a matter of course. But Hume thought chiefly of civil law, Smith of criminal. (2) They both talked about the *origin* of justice. They thought of themselves as giving causal explanation, in terms of psychology and sociology. Nevertheless, although they talked of origins, some of their evidence undoubtedly helps conceptual clarification. Hume's imaginary and real situations of utopia and of war point to limiting conditions in our use of the concept of justice. Smith's comparison of reactions to the sentinel and to a murderer highlights the difference between justification by utility and justification by desert.

Few people will deny Hume's contention that laws about property (or indeed any system of law) come into being because they are useful. And I think few people will deny Adam Smith's contention that the concept of punishment develops from feelings of resentment and the desire to retaliate. Hume and Smith were not really opposing each other here. The one was talking about the origins of civil laws of property, and was criticizing Locke's notion of a natural right to property. The other was talking about the origins of the *method of enforcing* a system of criminal law. But the Lectures on Jurisprudence show that Smith used his theory of sympathy and the impartial spectator to account also for the origins of the civil law of property. He said that the right to property by occupation depends on the sympathetic approval of an impartial spectator, and that the right to property by accession (e.g. to the produce of land or animals acquired by purchase) 'is not so much founded in it's utility as in the impropriety of not joining it to that object on which it has a dependance'.[8] I do not think that Smith's theory of propriety (sympathetic approval by an impartial spectator) has any real explanatory power when applied to property rights. For instance, he discussed Locke's example of acquiring property in the fruit that one has picked, and agreed that the right of ownership begins with the act of picking the fruit; but he did not follow Locke's argument that a natural right arises from having mixed with the earth the labour of one's body. Smith took the more customary view of natural law jurists that property rights are all acquired or 'adventitious', not natural. His argument for saying that ownership of the fruit begins with picking it was simply that an impartial spectator would sympathize with the fruit picker's resentment if some sly cad seized the fruit after it was picked but not if he darted in and snatched it while the first picker's hand was on the way. Smith's doctrine of the impartial spectator does no more here than repeat, in a roundabout way, that we think a right is violated in the one instance and not in the other. In the case of punishment, however, Smith is more impressive, both because he made use of his account of the double sympathy that constitutes the sense of merit, and because he was alive to psychological differences in real life cases which come before the courts.

What are the problems which the concept of justice raises for utilitarianism? I see them as follows: (1) It is difficult to dispose of the concept of desert in terms of utility when considering the justification of punishment, though not difficult in the case of reward. (2) The obligation to keep promises, and more generally to keep faith, does not seem to depend entirely on consequences. (3) A principle of equality, which is accepted by democrats (including democratic utilitarians—'Everybody to count for one'), is an addition to, not a consequence of, the principle of maximizing happiness, and sometimes the two principles can conflict. (4) All three of the considerations referred to above, and others also, exemplify the general point that a major function of the concept of justice is to express and defend the value of individual persons rather than the value of pleasure or happiness as such.

Where did Hume and Adam Smith stand in relation to these four points?

(1) *Desert*. Adam Smith's case against the utilitarian account of justice rested largely, though not entirely, on the difficulty about punishment. I have suggested that he did not press the objection far enough and that he perhaps conceded too much to Hume. In making the latter remark I was thinking of Hume's general thesis that justice depends on utility. For if we concentrate on the justice

of punishment, it is not easy to say where Hume stood. One passage in the *Enquiry*[9] suggests a utilitarian view but not unequivocally. A couple of brief passages in the *Treatise*[10] indicate some support for a view that is retributive, at least in part. However that may be, Hume's discussions of the relation of justice to utility barely glance at the justice of punishment.

(2) *Promises*. Hume is brilliant on the obligation of promises, and though nagging doubts may remain on the more general issue of keeping faith with other persons as a difficulty for utilitarianism, nobody can complain that Hume did not face the problems raised by promises. Adam Smith on the other hand evidently saw no problem. The subject was not even mentioned in the *Moral Sentiments*. The Lectures on Jurisprudence criticized the social contract theory of allegiance and of course dealt extensively with the law of contract; but on the obligation of promises Smith simply distinguished a promise from a declaration of intention and said that the obligation depends on 'the reasonable expectation produced by a promise', which he defined as 'a declaration of your desire that the person for whom you promise should depend on you for the performance of it'.[11] Professor Neil MacCormick has noted[12] that Adam Smith's view resembles his own theory that the obligation of a promise depends on the more general obligation which arises from having induced reliance. MacCormick contrasted his theory with the now popular view of promises which is essentially derived from Hume. He also suggested (but not very convincingly and perhaps not with conviction) that his account could be accommodated within utilitarianism just as well as the popular view which we owe to Hume, J. L. Austin, and John Searle. Adam Smith's brief account does indeed look similar to MacCormick's. There is, however, no evidence that Smith criticized Hume's theory of promises, that he regarded his brief definition as an alternative superior to Hume's view, or that he had any thoughts at all about the consistency or inconsistency of either with a utilitarian theory of cthics.[13]

(3) *Equality*. In the *Enquiry*[14] Hume considered briefly the idea that one conception of justice calls for equality. He confined himself to the extreme suggestion of a *perfect* equality of goods and, not surprisingly, dismissed it as impractical. Earlier in the *Enquiry*[15] he said that in a famine people would not think it 'criminal or

M

injurious' to make an equal distribution of bread without regard to property rights. Thomas Reid[16] fairly enough retorted that the equal distribution would be *required* by justice. Such an idea seems not to have crossed Hume's mind. He argued[17] that justice *presupposes* a measure of equality (of strength) in those to whom its rules apply, but this is not relevant to the notion that justice *calls for* equality where it does not exist—e.g. between men and women; Hume was content to record the fact that in many societies women are virtually in the position of slaves. Adam Smith was no more sensitive than Hume to an equalitarian conception of justice. In his youth he wrote enthusiastically of our tendency to admire 'the rich and the great'. In his old age he modified his view. He still thought that admiration of the rich and the great, with contempt for the poor and the weak, was both natural and socially useful; but he also thought it corrupted the moral sentiments, which approve of admiration only for the wise and the good, and of contempt only for the foolish and the bad. That is to say, he became more sensitive to the tension between social and moral stratification, but he was always a stratifier, never a leveller.

(4) *Individuals*. Adam Smith showed some awareness of this point when he said that concern for individuals does not depend on concern for society. Hume said a little, in the last paragraph of appendix iii to the *Enquiry*, about considering the position of the individual. He held that *after* the laws of justice are fixed from a regard to general utility, a *secondary* consideration which causes us to blame breaches of these laws is disapproval of the harm done to individuals. It is bound to be secondary, he argued, because the idea of violating an individual's rights presupposes laws of property, and these must be established for reasons of interest, as he had previously explained. This argument of Hume's is faulty. In the *Treatise* Hume distinguished 'three different species of goods which we are possess'd of; the internal satisfaction of our minds, the external advantages of our body, and the enjoyment of such possessions as we have acquir'd by our industry and good fortune'.[18] *Property* concerns the third of these. But a man can be injured in respect of reputation and body as well as in respect of property.[19] In the simplest of societies laws protecting people from personal injury are at least as basic as laws protecting property. Adam Smith said that 'the most sacred laws of justice' are those

which guard life and person, followed in order of importance by those which guard property and then by those which guard the rights of contract.[20]

Some scholars nowadays seem to think that the difficulties which utilitarianism faces over the concept of justice are resolved by substituting 'rule-utilitarianism' for 'act-utilitarianism'. Hume's account of justice is a form of rule-utilitarianism, and a suggestion of such a view is found also in Hutcheson's definition of rights in terms of universal practices. Both Hutcheson and Hume were thinking of the rules of law, which are indeed applied universally even though the result in individual cases is sometimes absurd. 'Hard cases make bad law', it is said. The justification commonly given is 'certainty', i.e. of predicting what the courts will decide. It is a utilitarian justification in that the advantages of certainty are held to outweigh the injustice of applying the rules inflexibly to hard cases. Outside the law, however, nobody in his senses thinks that the utility of rules requires inflexible adherence to them in hard cases. A good administrator is not the man bound by red tape; he is the man who knows what rules to make and who also knows when to break the rules. Apart from Kant, no deontologist thinks that the rules of promise-keeping or truth-telling should *never* be broken in the interests of utility. A rule-utilitarian presumably does not want us to be less flexible than we are.

Hume's version of rule-utilitarianism was intended to give a genetic explanation of why people approve of keeping a rule even in instances where it is contrary to utility. He said it is because of psychological association. Hume did not raise the question whether it is reasonable to act on such a form of approval if one has the choice either of following one's psychological bias or of aiming at maximum utility. It seems to me that a utilitarian ought to say that the only reasonable and right thing to do is to aim at utility. Does rule-utilitarianism counsel otherwise, and if so, why? If it does not, are we to suppose that modern rule-utilitarianism, like Hume, is giving a psychological explanation of how people do in fact judge, and not a criterion of how they should? In that event it would do well to look at Adam Smith's improvement on the psychology of Hume. I agree with Edward Westermarck that 'Adam Smith's *Theory of Moral Sentiments* is the most important contribution to moral psychology made by any British thinker'.[21]

11   Justice and Utility (II)

i

Utilitarianism has great attractions. It is a progressive philosophy that makes future improvement the criterion of all policy and decision; and it unifies within a simple framework the essential structure of ethics, economics, politics, and law. According to classical utilitarianism, the standard of morally right action is the increase of happiness, or the decrease of unhappiness, as much as possible for as many people as possible—'the greatest happiness of the greatest number'. Most people, with the help of education, are capable of following ethical aims to a certain extent in private life, but it is foolish to expect this in much of their action that affects the life of society generally. For the most part the average man acts with a view to his own private interest. The general concern of the classical utilitarians, Bentham and his followers, was to explain that the function of law and government is to match up the normal motivation of self-interest with the attainment in practice of the ethical standard, the public interest.

In the field of economics the classical utilitarians followed Adam Smith in thinking that the working of the market produces a *natural* harmony of interests. Although each person in economic life aims at his own advantage, the net result of market forces is the best possible advantage for society as a whole. Government interference in the economy has the consequence of less efficiency, a lesser total national product. So their recipe for economics was laissez-faire, complete liberty. In other aspects of social life, however, the utilitarians thought that there is *not* a natural harmony of interests. The whole point of having a system of law and government is to deal with conflicts of interest that need to be controlled. The purpose of government is to create an *artificial* harmony of interests, and it does this by means of the system of law.

According to Bentham, all law depends on sanctions, and so we can best understand the function of law, as he thought of it, if we look at criminal law. Crimes are actions which are harmful to society and which it is practicable to control by means of the legal system. Such actions are commonly done for the sake of individual gain. What is harmful to society can be attractive to the individual. His private interest conflicts with public interest. The way to harmonize them is to make unattractive the anti-social action which appears to the individual to be attractive. The would-be thief is attracted by the pleasant prospect of using the money that he steals. The criminal law adds the unpleasant prospect of imprisonment and so deters the potential thief from doing an action that is harmful to society. The total consequences now make the action unattractive. The law with its sanctions produces an artificial harmony of private and public interest.

Utilitarianism, then, is both comprehensive and simple. It uses a simple standard with an obvious appeal, the promotion of general happiness, to explain and relate ethics, economics, politics, and law. It is a forward-looking doctrine, justifying things by reference to the future, and so it seems a progressive philosophy.

Nevertheless, as is well known, utilitarianism runs into severe difficulties, especially in ethical theory. Unless our ordinary moral intuitions are quite mistaken, there are many situations in which the right action is not the one that seems the most useful, and certainly its justification does not lie in an appeal to utility. Often the justification depends on the past, not the future. A promise ought to be kept because it has been undertaken as a promise, not because its results will contribute most to general happiness. No amount of useful consequences can justify the punishing of an innocent man; punishment is permissible only if he has done wrong. Obligations of gratitude, kinship, friendship, likewise depend essentially on the past rather than the future.

In the light of these objections, some utilitarians have drawn a distinction between act-utilitarianism and rule-utilitarianism. Act-utilitarianism is the straightforward theory that every right act is to be justified by its utility. Rule-utilitarianism is the theory that general moral rules are to be justified by their utility, but that individual right acts are to be done because they conform to a moral rule. According to rule-utilitarianism, a particular act that conforms to a moral rule should be adopted as the right one even if in this instance following the rule seems likely to produce less useful consequences than an alternative act.

It seems to me that rule-utilitarianism is an irrational theory. Of course all utilitarians have agreed that it is often sensible and right to follow ordinary moral rules because we can generally rely on their utility. But if it appears, in a particular instance, that following a rule will *not* produce the most useful results, why should a utilitarian follow it? A rule-utilitarian may try to argue that following the rule is *always* the most useful action, despite appearances to the contrary, because breaking the rule will weaken the system. To my mind this line of argument is implausible, but at least it is theoretically consistent with utilitarianism. It is so, however, simply because rule-utilitarianism has now collapsed into act-utilitarianism. The view is that each particular act of following the rule is after all the most useful one.

As a matter of history, rule-utilitarianism arose from reflection on rights. The concept of a right is basically a legal concept; so-called moral rights depend on analogy with legal rights. The rules of positive law apply universally, to all cases that fall under them. Legal rights, functioning as they do within the context of legal rules, likewise apply universally. Utilitarianism proper (as contrasted with Epicureanism) arose in a tradition of reflection that linked ethics with jurisprudence. Philosophers in that tradition who turned their attention to rights thought first and foremost of legal rights. So if they wanted to give a utilitarian account of rights, it had to be in terms of *universal rules*.

That this is true of Hume is well known. Hume is generally regarded as the founder of rule-utilitarianism. But the reason for Hume's rule-utilitarianism is not so generally noticed. He reaches rule-utilitarianism in giving an account of justice as an artificial virtue, and his conception of justice seems to be curiously narrow, being more or less equated with rights in relation to property. This curiosity can be explained, I believe, by reference to history. Hume's primary purpose in this part of his *Treatise of Human Nature* is to undermine the view of ethical rationalists (at this particular point he is thinking especially of Locke) that there is a natural right to property. He therefore sets out to show that the system of property rights, and of the obligation to respect them, is artificial. This system forms a very substantial part of the civil law, and the subject-matter of law was commonly described at that time (certainly in academic courses of moral philosophy) as 'justice'. So when Hume gives an account of 'justice', i.e. of property rights, in terms of utility and of a basic empiricism (by contrast with theories of absolute or 'natural' law discerned by reason), he has in mind the rules of civil law. It is not surprising, therefore, that he should think of his utilitarian theory as an explanation of universal rules, and not as an explanation of individual acts.

The characterization of 'justice' (the respect for property rights) as an 'artificial virtue' was an important innovation in Hume's ethics. But the idea of rule-utilitarianism as an explanation of laws and of rights did not originate with him. Here, as elsewhere in his ethical theory, Hume built on Francis Hutcheson. Hutcheson developed an explicit utilitarianism from his theory of moral sense and benevolence. The moral sense approves of benevolence; the degree of the approval varies directly with the breadth of the benevolence, so that universal benevolence is approved most of all. Hence the *'best'* action is that which 'procures the greatest happiness for the greatest numbers'.[1] The explicit principle of utilitarianism that thus emerges in Hutcheson is a principle of act-utilitarianism. But he immediately goes on to relate it to a utilitarian conception of law that takes in, 'not only the direct and natural effects of the actions themselves', but also the probability that an action may 'be made a precedent in unlike cases'.

And this is the reason, that many laws prohibit actions in general, even when some particular instances of those actions would be very useful; because an universal allowance of them, considering the mistakes men would probably fall into, would be more pernicious than an universal prohibition; . . .[2]

When Hutcheson gives an analysis of the concept of rights in a later section, he again writes of the utility of a universal rule; and this is because, like Hume after him, he takes it for granted that in talking of rights he is talking of law. He defines rights as follows:

Whenever it appears to us, that a faculty of doing, demanding, or possessing any thing, universally allowed in certain circumstances, would in the whole tend to the general good, we say, that one in such circumstances has a right to do, possess, or demand that thing.[3]

It is perhaps worth remarking *en passant* that Kant's concept of universalizing moral rules, in his first formulation of the Categorical Imperative, depends on analogy with the law. When Kant says that a necessary condition for the morality of an action is that the *maxim* (or rule) of the action can be willed to be a universal law, he is comparing morals with legislation, and the comparison is persuasive. But suppose you are wrestling with some difficult moral dilemma, with a conflict of obligations, and you decide, with some misgivings, that so far as *you* are concerned, obligation *A* must take precedence over obligation *B* in these particular circumstances: is it so convincing to say either that you must be ready to universalize your decision or that you can properly compare such moral decision with legislation? If an analogy with law is to be sought, is it not better sought in the judgement of a *court*, not in the resolution of a *legislature*? The judgement of a court that an ambiguous case should be determined by following rule or precedent *A* rather than *B* is indeed liable to be treated as itself a precedent for the future, i.e. as a rule to be applied universally to all like cases; but the pragmatic reasons that make this useful in the administration of law do not, I think, apply so obviously to the moral conduct of private life.

As with Kantian, so with utilitarian ethics. It is proper to compare general moral rules with rules of law, but the analogy breaks down when it comes to the morality of some individual acts that do not conform to the general tendency of their kind. If a particular action seems clearly *not* to be the most useful one open to the agent, why should a utilitarian say it is right? Because actions of that kind are *usually* useful, replies the adherent of rule-utilitarianism. But where is the sense, in terms of utility, of slavishly following a rule because it is generally useful, although you feel confident that in this instance it will not be useful? Rule-utilitarianism makes sense in an account of law because one can reasonably say that, although the direct effects of following the rule in one instance are harmful, the indirect effects of breaking the rule are likely to be more harmful. Law depends so much on 'certainty', on confidence that precedents will be followed, that one can make a really convincing case for the genuine *utility* of applying the rules universally, without exception for hard cases. In morals there is no such convincing case. That is why so many people jib at the rigidity of Kant's own interpretation of the Categorical Imperative. That is why a number of people jib at R. M. Hare's adherence to universalization for all moral decisions. And that is why rule-utilitarianism, as a theory of *morals*, is irrational unless it collapses into act-utilitarianism.

Hutcheson and Hume, the originators of rule-utilitarianism, did not intend it to be understood as a theory applying to the whole of morals. When they applied it to rights (or, in Hume's parlance, to 'justice'), they were thinking of the law, where it makes very good sense.

ii

Professor H. L. A. Hart, in his British Academy lecture on Bentham, says that Bentham's treatment of rights 'betrays' a 'nervousness', a sense that 'the idea of rights would always excite a peculiarly strong suspicion that the doctrine of utility was not an adequate expression of men's moral ideas and political ideals'.[4] Hart goes on to examine Bentham's analysis of rights and pinpoints its weaknesses with the criticism that Bentham neglects the *distributive* character of rights. By this expression Hart means that a right pertains essentially to the individual who has it. 'He is not merely one of an aggregate or class who are likely to benefit . . .'; 'the person said to have the right is not viewed merely as a member of a class who as a class may be indiscriminately benefited . . .' Hart goes on to say that 'Bentham's *reductio ad absurdum* of non legal rights also fails because it too neglects, though in a different way, the essentially distributive character of a right'. Moral rights 'must refer to the present properties or past actions of the individuals who are said to have' them.[5]

Hart prefaces his criticism with the remark that Bentham's mistakes on rights 'were inherited by Mill who struggled against them with only partial success'.[6] He is referring to Chapter 5 of Mill's *Utilitarianism*.[7] It seems to me at least misleading, if not itself a mistake, to say that Mill there inherits Bentham's mistakes on rights. The crucial point about that chapter of *Utilitarianism* is the reference of justice, including rights, to assignable individuals.

N

Having seized on this in his *analysis* of justice, Mill then forgets about it in his *explanation*. But that is an error of his own commission, not one that he inherited from Bentham.

The subject of Mill's chapter is 'the connection between justice and utility', not simply the connection between rights and utility. Mill at first subsumes rights under justice as one species among others, and it is the more general concept of justice that he takes to be (in his first paragraph) 'one of the strongest obstacles' or (in his last paragraph) 'the only real difficulty in the utilitarian theory of morals'.[8] In this I agree with Mill's first thoughts. The scope of justice is wider than that of rights, and the obstacle to utilitarianism comes from the wider concept, not from that of rights alone. I also think that the nature of the obstacle is best brought out by talking, as Mill does, of reference to the *individual* rather than of a *distributive* character. If distribution is contrasted with aggregation, then certainly one can say that the principles of justice are distributive. But since a distinction has traditionally and usefully been drawn between 'distributive justice' and 'retributive justice' (the latter meaning the requital of good for good as well as of evil for evil), the adjective 'distributive' can mislead if applied to justice as a whole. The point that Hart wishes to make against Bentham is better made by contrasting the individual with the group than by contrasting distribution with aggregation.

Mill's strategy in Chapter 5 of *Utilitarianism* is to argue that while our feelings of justice have their *origin* in the natural feeling of vengeance, that feeling then becomes moralized, and accordingly can only be *justified*, by the thought of utility.

In order to show this, Mill first gives an analysis of the concept of justice. It is applied to several kinds of things, and Mill lists these in order to find out what is the common attribute in them all that allows the same term to be applied to them. His list has six constituents: we use the term justice of legal rights, moral rights, desert, keeping faith (i.e. the fulfilment of promises and contracts, and the payment of debts), impartiality, and equality. It is not easy at first sight to see any common character in all of these six notions; so Mill turns to etymology and concludes from this that justice always has some reference to the sanctions of law.

He may be right, but his argument is poor. He acknowledges that etymology is 'slight evidence' of the present meaning of an idea, but adds that etymology is 'the very best evidence of how it sprang up'.[9] No doubt—provided that you can be confident of your etymology. Mill's excursion into the etymology of justice runs as follows. '*Justum* is a form of *jussum*, that which has been ordered. Δίκαιον comes directly from δίκη, a suit at law. *Recht* . . . is synonymous with law. . . . *La justice* . . . is the established term for judicature.'[9] He goes on to say that conformity to law 'consituted the entire idea' of justice among the Hebrews, up to the birth of Christianity; but he evidently did not ask any of his friends whether the actual language of the Old Testament bears this out.

Mill's confident assertion that the Latin *iustum* comes from *iussum* is certainly an error; *iustum* comes from *ius*. (Philologists have indeed suggested the virtual converse of what Mill says—that *iubeo* comes from *ius habeo*, but they do not pretend to any confidence on that matter.) Now it is more than doubtful whether the Latin *ius*, the Greek δίκη, and the German word *Recht*, were at first purely legal ideas with no moral element. I should suspect that there was no clear distinction between legal and moral outlooks in the earliest uses of these words. So far as the usage of the Old Testament is concerned, a distinction is already present and it in fact goes contrary to Mill's assumption. The two most common terms for law in the Old Testament (*hok* or *hukkah*, and *mishpat*) are commonly translated 'statute' and 'judgement'. Their etymological associations show clearly that they refer respectively to published (literally 'engraved') prescription and to decision by judges. (Neither of these terms is the one which is applied to the Five Books of Moses as a whole and which is commonly translated 'the Law'. That word, *torah*, means a pointing out, and so instruction or doctrine, not law in any literal sense.) As contrasted with these words for statutes and judgements, the words that are translated as 'justice' and 'just' (*tsedek*, *tsadik*) are remarkably close in their usage to the terms for justice in languages more familiar to Europeans. The moral connotation of the words is clear and emphatic. In so far as they are used of law and of a ruler or judge (whether human or divine), they tend to be limited to specific classes of judgements or actions that accord with our ordinary concept of justice, namely those that concern punishment and reward, the fulfilment of promises, and the having of a right. Outside these legal or quasi-legal uses, the words tend to spill over into moral areas that we should regard as outside the scope of justice, such as kindness, temperance, and the love of truth. The fact that the biblical concept of justice is firmly moral and not simply legal is of particular significance for us because our modern concept of justice has been more influenced by the Bible than by the thought of Greece and Rome.

Mill knew more about the thought of Greece and Rome than about the Bible. He recognized that, despite his supposed etymology, the Greeks and the Romans were capable of thinking that a law could be unjust. And of course he had previously noted that the concept of justice is applied in non-legal as well as in legal contexts. So he concludes that, while justice and injustice originally meant conformity to and breach of law, they have come to mean conformity to and breach of what ought to be law, or at least what ought to be sanctioned by punishment.

But then, it turns out, the discussion of the etymology of words for justice was useless; for Mill recalls his own particular view that the meaning he has assigned to justice applies to the whole of morality. For Mill, the sphere of morality is the sphere of duty or right and wrong, and should be distinguished from the wider sphere of the good or desirable, of which it is one species among others. The good or desirable is always happiness, and the doctrine of utilitarianism, which commends happiness as the sole ultimate end, goes beyond morality. It covers 'the Art of Life, in its three departments, Morality, Prudence or Policy, and Aesthetics; the Right, the Expedient, and the Beautiful or Noble, in human conduct and works'.[10] Virtues that go beyond the requirements of strict duty are assigned by Mill to the category of aesthetics ('the beautiful or noble') and not to the category of morality. Morality, then, is a species of the good or desirable, and justice is a sub-species of morality. Throughout the category of morality we speak of duties or obligations, of right and wrong, of what ought and ought not to be done. These words are all more forceful than the value terms which we are ready to use in the categories of prudence and aesthetics. They are more forceful, not simply in expressing our wishes and feelings with greater emphasis, but in expressing a desire that force might be applied, if necessary, to produce compliant conduct. In short, morality for Mill is that class of actions which we should wish to see enforced by the sanction of punishment for breaches.

This means that Mill's proposed definition of justice is too wide. It defines morality as a whole. How then is justice to be differentiated from the rest of morality? Justice, Mill says, is that part of morality which writers of the past have described by 'the ill-chosen expression', duties of perfect obligation, and in 'more precise language' as those duties which give rise to correlative rights in other persons.[11] Mill therefore comes to make justice co-extensive with moral rights, despite his earlier classification of moral rights as only one of six concepts to which the term 'justice' is applied. What seems to me more significant is that, in differentiating justice from morality, Mill refers several times to the position of *individual persons*. Justice, he says, involves 'the idea of a personal right—a claim on the part of one or more individuals'; injustice implies 'a wrong done, and some assignable person who is wronged'; justice implies something which 'some individual person can claim from us as his moral right'; by contrast, there is no moral right to generosity or beneficence, because 'we are not morally bound to practise those virtues towards any given individual'.[11] Mill states the conclusion of his analysis as a recognition that 'the two essential ingredients in the sentiment of justice are, the desire to punish a person who has done harm, and the knowledge or belief that there is some definite individual or individuals to whom harm has been done'.[12]

Having completed his analysis, Mill proceeds to explanation. The odd thing is that his explanation is confined to the first of 'the two essential ingredients'. He tells us that the desire to punish arises out of the natural impulse 'to resent, and to repel or retaliate' harm which is done to us or to those near and dear to us. This natural sentiment is moralized when it is directed by social sympathy towards the interest of society instead of being confined to our own narrow interest. When he comes to apply this account to the various manifestations of justice, Mill does not find it all plain sailing, and this is because it is not so simple to assimilate the whole of justice to the right of protection from harm. Mill has to say that the injustice of breaking a promise, and of ingratitude or failing to reward good desert, consists in disappointing a reasonable expectation, that such disappointing is a form of harming, and that it stirs resentment comparable with the resentment caused by direct injury. When Mill comes to impartiality and equality, he is in still greater difficulty. He at first tries to deal with these connected concepts as a special case of requiting desert (equal treatment for equal desert). But then he moves to the different ground of arguing that equal distribution is 'a direct emanation' of the utilitarian principle of maximizing happiness. Of course it is no such thing. Mill notes Herbert Spencer's objection to the suggestion and quite misses the point in his reply.[13]

However, my main concern is not with the fact that Mill cannot easily bring all six of his species of just acts within his explanation of justice as the desire to retaliate, moralized by sympathy. I want to ask instead, what has happened to the *second* of the 'two essential ingredients of justice', the reference to assignable individuals? Mill seems to have forgotten about that.

There is one paragraph which suggests that Mill has not so much forgotten as failed to grasp the significance of his own point. Quite early in his explanation, having stated that the desire to punish arises from the desire for vengeance and is then moralized by sympathy with the interest of society as a whole, he considers an objection.

It is no objection against this doctrine to say, that when we feel our sentiment of justice outraged, we are not thinking of society at large, or of any collective interest, but only of the individual case.[14]

Mill's answer to this objection presupposes that 'the individual case' means *our own* individual case. 'It is common enough', he says, to feel resentment for oneself, but a man who has that feeling does not have a concern for justice 'if he is regarding the act solely as it affects him individually'; he must 'feel that he is asserting a rule which is for the benefit of others as well as for his own'.[15]

This is thoroughly perverse. The objection that 'when we feel our sentiment of justice outraged', we are thinking, not of society at large, but of 'the individual case', does not mean that we are thinking of *our own* individual case. It means that we are thinking of the individual case of a Socrates, or the individual case of a Dreyfus, that we are asserting the claims of an innocent individual against the general interest of the society. Of course we are appealing to a rule 'which is for the benefit of others' as well as for our own. The point of the objection is that the rule insists on the benefit of those others as *individuals*, in contrast to the general benefit of society at large.

This does not mean that there is a total opposition between justice and utility. Mill is quite right when he says that 'people are in general willing enough to allow, that objectively the dictates of Justice coincide with a part of the field of General Expediency'.[16] Yet it remains true that justice and utility can and do conflict quite frequently. When they do, the principles of justice proclaim the rights of the individual. Mill's analysis of the concept of justice led him to see this, but the heritage of utilitarianism blinkered his perception and caused him to miss the significance of his own insight.

Notes

1 Equality and Equity

1 I use the word 'obligation' here to mean the same as Sir David Ross's expression '*prima facie* duty'.
2 *Collected Papers* (1911), vol. i, p. 154.
3 p. 131.
4 Address on 'Social Equality', in *Social Rights and Duties* (1896), vol. i, p. 177.
5 p. 185.
6 p. 184.
7 Published by the Manchester Statistical Society, 1944.
8 'Morally right' is used here in the sense of 'obligatory'. Sometimes the adjective 'right' is used so as to mean 'not wrong' and so to include both the morally right and the morally neutral.
9 As usually stated, though it could be stated as a claim of special need. Opening the House of Commons Debate on the demobilization plan, Lt.-Col. John Profumo based the claim of those serving overseas on the special hardship involved in the prolonged and uninterrupted separation of father from children.
10 This does not of course mean that the obligation to help the needy is derived from the principle of equity or that of equality. The point is that *discrimination* in favour of the needy is justified by equity, and justified as supporting equality, not as opposing it.
11 This double claim of the disabled ex-serviceman caused a number of Members of Parliament, when the Disabled Persons (Employment) Bill was considered (again towards the end of the Second World War), to forget that other disabled men also have the special claim of need. The Minister of Labour, Ernest Bevin, resisted attempts to give priority of employment to disabled ex-servicemen only and insisted that all disabled men, from whatever cause their disability arose, should have the priority, though he agreed that if it were impossible to find work for all of them the disabled ex-serviceman would have the stronger claim.
12 Some would say that the principle involved is a moral claim to self-development and not the obligation of beneficence. At any rate it is not the principle of equity.
13 The State does not subsidize scientific research for its own sake. Those who value knowledge for its own sake may provide money for pursuing this end, but subsidies from the public purse have a utilitarian purpose, to benefit the public.

2 Freedom and Fair Shares: the Issue of an Election

1 This is the first part of an essay on 'The Issues' of the General Election of 1950, as shown in the Glasgow constituencies. It was originally published together with essays by other contributors on different aspects of that election. All the essays arose from a survey of the election in Glasgow conducted by members of the University of Glasgow. I have retained the titles (e.g. 'Mr. Churchill') that those concerned had at the time.

3 Justice and Liberty

1 For a fuller discussion of Plato's concept of justice, see Essay 5, below.
2 1st ed. (1937), p. 667; apparently omitted in the revised edition.
3 See Essay 2, above.
4 *The Right and the Good* (1930), pp. 21, 26-7, 138.
5 Cf., e.g., E. F. Carritt, *Ethical and Political Thinking* (1947), ch. ix.
6 Cf. W. G. Maclagan, 'Punishment and Retribution' (*Philosophy*, July 1939), § v.
7 *Agrarian Justice;* quoted by F. W. Maitland in 'Liberty and Equality' (*Collected Papers* (1911), vol. i, p. 148).

4 Tensions between Equality and Freedom

1 See Essay 9, below, for a more detailed discussion of Reverse Discrimination, especially as considered by the U.S. Supreme Court in the cases of *DeFunis* and *Bakke*.

5 Conservative and Prosthetic Justice

1 Elaborated in *Moral Judgement* (1955), ch. vii, § 6.
2 I have been asked whether the scope of justice is not narrower than that of rights in general, for we should not say that, e.g., the right to be told the truth is a part of justice. I think the answer is that justice is co-extensive with rights, and that the supposed counter-example induces doubts simply because of the misleading form in which it is phrased. A man does not have a right to be told all the truths that his companions know; he might rather claim a right to be spared the boredom of such revelations. Nor does he have a right to be given a truthful answer to all his questions, for some of the questions might be unwarranted intrusion into the private affairs of other people. He has a right not to be deliberately deceived, and this is what is properly meant when we speak of a right to be told the truth. When a man is deliberately deceived, it would be apt for him to say to the deceiver: 'You have not dealt fairly with me.' That is, a breach of the right in question is a breach of fairness or justice.

3 This short section contains the kernel of my view of justice. It is short because it simply summarizes an account which I have already given elsewhere (Essay 3, § iv, above, and *Moral Judgement*, ch. vii, § 5).

6 Chaim Perelman on Justice

1 In Chaim Perelman, *The Idea of Justice and the Problem of Argument* (1963). My references are to this version of the essay.
2 p. 57.
3 *The New Rhetoric* (English translation, 1969), §§ 27, 52; *The Idea of Justice and the Problem of Argument*, pp. 86, 119.
4 *The Idea of Justice*, pp. 6–10.
5 p. 18.
6 p. 24.
7 Essay 5, above; cf. *Problems of Political Philosophy* (1970; revised ed., 1976), ch. vii, pp. 170–2.
8 The Practice Statement begins: 'Their Lordships regard the use of precedent as an indispensable foundation upon which to decide what is the law and its application to individual cases. It provides at least some degree of certainty upon which individuals can rely in the conduct of their affairs, as well as a basis for orderly development of legal rules.' Cf. Sir Rupert Cross, *Precedent in English Law*, 3rd ed. (1977), p. 109.
9 *Davis* v. *Johnson*, [1979] A.C. 264. The considered judgement of the House on this point was delivered by Lord Diplock at 326: 'In an appellate court of last resort a balance must be struck between the need on the one side for the legal certainty resulting from the binding effect of previous decisions, and, on the other side the avoidance of undue restriction on the proper development of the law.'

8 Taking Law Seriously

1 *The Concept of Law*, p. 96.
2 p. 199. My italics.
3 pp. 96, 151.
4 Quoted from Dworkin, *Taking Rights Seriously*, p. 23.
5 p. 24.
6 p. 26.
7 As reported in the *Daily Telegraph*, 9 May 1979.
8 Quoted from *The Times*, 20 January 1978.
9 *Introduction to English Law*, ed. 8 (1972), p. 142.
10 [1978] 2 W.L.R. 695, H.L.(E.)
11 i.e. legal gibberish.
12 At 713.
13 *Taking Rights Seriously*, p. 73.
14 For the point made in this paragraph, cf. Geoffrey Marshall, 'Posi-

tivism, Adjudication, and Democracy', Essay 7 in P. M. S. Hacker and J. Raz (eds.), *Law, Morality, and Society* (1977).
15 Cf. Essay 6, § iii, above.
16 *Introduction to English Law*, ed. 8, p. 12.
17 [1979] A.C. 264, at 326. Cf. Essay 6, note 9, above.
18 *Taking Rights Seriously*, p. 172.
19 p. 198.
20 Cf. the judgement of Sir George Baker, quoted on p. 120 above: 'This court cannot and *should not* . . . permit her to achieve an end by the course of conduct she had pursued.'
21 p. vii.
22 My criticism of Dworkin on this score is developed in Essay 9, § v, below.
23 p. 264.
24 *On Liberty and Liberalism: the case of John Stuart Mill* (1974).
25 p. 262.

9 Reverse Discrimination

1 W. Friedmann, *Law in a Changing Society* (1959), p. 24.
2 *Regents of University of California* v. *Bakke*, 98 S.Ct. 2733 (1978).
3 Cf. Brennan J. in the Bakke case, at 2774.
4 *Davis* v. *Johnson*, [1979] A.C. 264: (C.A.), Lord Denning M.R. at 276–7; (H.L.(E.)), Viscount Dilhorne at 337 and Lord Scarman at 349–50.
5 Cf. note 26 to the opinion of Powell J. in the U.S. Supreme Court's judgement (at 2748).
6 Note 14, at 2744.
7 Note 45, at 2758.
8 At 2810.
9 At 2811.
10 At 2815.
11 At 2809. My italics.
12 *DeFunis* v. *Odegaard*, 94 S.Ct. 1704 (1974).
13 Ronald Dworkin, 'Reverse Discrimination', in *Taking Rights Seriously* (1977), pp. 224–5.
14 At 2747–8.
15 At 2748.
16 At 2763.
17 Note 52.
18 Brennan J. *et al.*, at 2794.
19 The paper was first published in the *New York Review of Books*; republished, under the title 'Reverse Discrimination', in Ronald Dworkin, *Taking Rights Seriously* (1977); and republished again, with some modification, under the title 'DeFunis and Sweatt', in Richard Bronaugh (ed.), *Philosophical Law* (1978).
20 *Taking Rights Seriously*, p. 227. I note with interest that this sentence

does not appear in the version printed in *Philosophical Law*, because the paragraph which contained it has been largely rewritten. But the substance of Dworkin's conclusion remains unaltered. See next note.

21 *Taking Rights Seriously*, p. 239. In *Philosophical Law*, p. 71, the distinction between 'utilitarian' and 'ideal' is replaced by one between 'economic' and 'noneconomic', but this seems to be purely a change of nomenclature, not a change of view.

22 *Taking Rights Seriously*, p. 232; *Philosophical Law*, p. 55.

23 p. 228, note.

24 p. 57.

25 p. 60 and note 5 on p. 73.

26 On 'distinct' and 'important', cf. the passages cited in notes 23-5 above. In *Philosophical Law*, p. 57, the mention of 'rights so important' is followed by a reference to 'absolute' rights, apparently meaning the same kind of thing.

27 *Philosophical Law*, p. 57.

28 *Taking Rights Seriously*, p. 227.

29 At 2764.

30 At 2753.

31 At 2806.

32 I have been told that a sociological survey suggested that two-thirds of university teachers in the U.S.A. are opposed to special admissions programmes.

10 Justice and Utility (I)

1 N. Kemp Smith, *The Philosophy of David Hume* (1941).

2 III.ii.2; ed. Selby-Bigge, p. 497.

3 *Treatise*, III.ii.1; ed. Selby-Bigge, p. 481.

4 Ed. Selby-Bigge, § 257.

5 *TMS* (=*Theory of Moral Sentiments*), II.ii.3.9.

6 *TMS*, II.ii.3.11.

7 *LJ* (=*Lectures on Jurisprudence*, ed. Meek, Raphael, and Stein, 1978), (B) 182; cf. (A) 91-2.

8 *LJ*, (B) 152; cf. (A) 64.

9 *Enquiry concerning Morals*, III.i; ed. Selby-Bigge, § 148.

10 *Treatise*, II.iii.2 and III.iii.1; ed. Selby-Bigge, pp. 410-11 and 591.

11 *LJ*, (B) 175-6; cf. (A) 42-4.

12 *Aristotelian Society Supp. Vol.* 46 (1972), p. 78, *n.* 9.

13 A writer who did criticize Hume's account of the obligation of promises and argue for the reliance theory as a superior alternative was Henry Home, Lord Kames, in *Essays on the Principles of Morality and Natural Religion* (1751), Part I, essay ii, ch. 7.

14 III.ii; ed. Selby-Bigge, § 155.

15 III.i; ed. Selby-Bigge, § 147.

16 *Essays on the Active Powers*, v. 5.

17 *Enquiry*, III.i.; ed. Selby-Bigge, § 152.

18 *Treatise*, III.ii.2; ed. Selby-Bigge, p. 487.
19 Cf. Adam Smith, *LJ*, (B) 6; (A) 12.
20 *TMS*, II.ii.2.2.
21 *Ethical Relativity* (1932), p. 71.

11   Justice and Utility (II)

1 Francis Hutcheson, *Inquiry concerning Virtue*, III.8; in D. D. Raphael, *British Moralists 1650–1800* (1969), § 333.
2 *British Moralists*, § 334.
3 *Inquiry*, VII.6; *British Moralists*, § 353.
4 H. L. A. Hart, 'Bentham', *Proceedings of the British Academy*, 48 (1962); reprinted in B. Parekh (ed.), *Jeremy Bentham* (1974), Essay 4. The quotation is from § iv; in Parekh, p. 85.
5 In Parekh, pp. 87, 87–8, 88.
6 p. 87.
7 pp. 91–2.
8 J. S. Mill, *Utilitarianism*, ch. v; in Everyman ed., pp. 38, 59–60; in Fontana ed., pp. 296, 321.
9 Everyman, p. 43; Fontana, p. 302.
10 J. S. Mill, *System of Logic*, VI.xii.6.
11 Everyman, p. 46; Fontana, p. 305.
12 Everyman, p. 47; Fontana, p. 306.
13 Everyman, p. 58; Fontana, p. 319.
14 Everyman, p. 48; Fontana, pp. 307–8.
15 Everyman, p. 48; Fontana, p. 308.
16 Everyman, p. 39; Fontana, p. 297.

Index